The Breakthrough Point

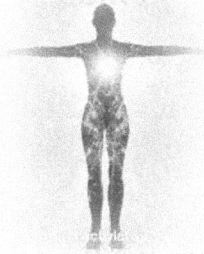

The Breakthrough Point

A Spiritual Activist's Guide to Thriving in a
Modern World

Lynn Woodland

Waterside Press
Cardiff, CA

Printed in the United States of America

First Printing, 2018

ISBN-13: 978-1-947637-96-2 print edition
ISBN-13: 978-1-947637-97-9 ebook edition

Waterside Press
2055 Oxford Ave
Cardiff, CA 92007
www.waterside.com

Contents

Introduction

A number of experts, in a variety of fields and for different reasons, predicted that 2016 would be a game-changing year. I suggest here that 2016 marked a tipping point in an evolutionary call to Unity that has been building for years. As a way of articulating this evolutionary pull, I have tied it to a spiritual event, the Harmonic Convergence, which took place in 1987. I've used the filter of astrological wisdom to interpret some of the marker events of evolutionary change since 1987. A better astrologer than I might have a far more in-depth and informative analysis on this. I have simply used a single astrological indicator because it so compellingly connects dots, tying together global benchmark events that might otherwise appear random and unrelated to an evolutionary trend toward peaceful cooperation.

But this isn't a book about the Harmonic Convergence or astrology, or changes happening in obscure spiritual realms that only the most sensitive can perceive. Rather, it's an in-depth look at a new operating model for humanity that is integrally tied to a new evolutionary order. This is no utopian fantasy; it's a strong global trend that has made its way into major areas of science, business, technology and culture.

Still, amidst exciting indications of a world coming together, it's hard not to feel buffeted by a world that's coming apart: unprecedented political turmoil, escalating terrorism, environmental crises, endless wars, deepening racial and ideological divides, and financial uncertainties, to name just a few modern-day stressors.

This book offers a path for aligning with the new operating model of our times and catching the wave of wonderful possibilities that come with evolution, instead of being drawn into the fear and breakdown of an old way of being. I'm not offering here my own trademarked plan for positive living, as you will find in many other books. This new model is nothing mysterious; it's a trend that is all around, growing as quietly and inevitably as shoots of grass around the rubble of a fallen building. As soon as I lay it out, you will probably realize that you've been aware of it all along.

Simple though it may seem, if we don't learn to bring our lives into alignment with this new way of doing things, we will increasingly experience the stress and breakdown of living in a troubled world. Making the shift, both in practice and consciousness, enables undreamed breakthroughs in our personal lives and in the world.

The spiritual exercises here evolve power-of-consciousness practices in accordance with the new operating model, offering a radical departure from more familiar approaches, and continuing the adventure in consciousness begun in my previous book, *Holding a Butterfly*, (formerly titled *Making Miracles*).

Many of these are essentially guided meditations and begin with a suggestion to enter a quiet, reflective state of mind. If you are not familiar with meditation, this can be done quite simply by assuming a comfortable position (but not so comfortable that you will easily fall asleep), and then watching the inhalation and exhalation of your breath, inhaling deeply from your abdomen and exhaling just as deeply, letting your breath find a smooth, slow, comfortable rhythm. As you do this, notice your body and allow any points of tension to relax. Several moments of this are often enough to slow your heart rate and quiet your mind in order to make the most of these exercises. They are best done when you have some quiet time to yourself.

Some are a bit long and, for best results, you can either read them slowly in a quiet, reflective state, make a recording to listen to with your eyes closed, or listen to the recordings of these exercises that are available for free on my website, www.lynnwoodland.com, or you can purchase a CD or download.

Perhaps the best way of all to experience this book is with a study group, where you can discuss the chapters and do the exercises together, with one person reading the meditations aloud.

For those of you who have read *Holding a Butterfly*, I thank you for coming back! You will once again find in this book an opportunity to join in a global community experiment to share the world-changing consciousness of love, and to experience heightened peace of mind, quality of life, and joy. You will also find a deeper exploration of the times we're in, why they are both dire and wonderful, and why we can no longer hold on to the way things were. There is a *single* path beyond the breakdown of our times and it is one that we must walk together—and only together. This is how we not only survive but breakthrough to new realms of thriving. Together, anything becomes possible and, even in the midst of the crises of our world, this is a wonderful thing!

And before I release you to the book proper, let me just answer a question before it has a chance to arise in your mind: why so much social commentary in a book of spiritual practices? Having traveled in circles that identify as "New Age," "Metaphysical," "New Thought," or "Spiritual but not Religious" for most of my life, I've noticed how often people in my spiritual circles, when asked their thoughts on world events, respond that they don't pay attention. I understand this. For those of us intent on meditating into a peaceful state, the messiness of the world is a rough and crude vibration. For those of us who have turned to spirituality as a balm for our heightened sensitivities to the world around us, politics and world affairs can be the worst of allergens. And some of us have simply given up because we don't see anything changing from the top down, and so have immersed ourselves in the world of higher consciousness.

As I say, I understand. But I hope to convince you that while, at one time, it may have been necessary to tune out, these times are like no other and the new energy coming in demands our involvement. It's time to tune back in because change can come more easily now than ever to those who are attentive enough to reach for it.

And now, let's reach!

Section I:

Changing Times

In the morning, in the rise up, there's a bridge from all that's been

In the dawning, the vines are pushing through the pavement

We were born of burning hearts, we are tearing off the reigns

From the ground up, we will build it

From the clouds above we'll rain it

From the crowd up we will raise it

From the ground up...

~ Ayla Nereo ("From the Ground Up" lyrics)

Chapter 1: Let the Journey Begin

Quiet your mind for a moment and let your attention float free. Take a deep breath or two to help you transition to a soft, open mental state...

Now imagine that you are at a turning point in your life, though you may not realize it yet. (You don't need to believe this, just imagine.) Recall other turning points where everything changed in the direction of your highest good. Perhaps you met your significant other or had an opportunity come to you that changed everything. Maybe you decided to move or take a new job and the change had a huge, positive impact on your life. Maybe it was when you left home for the first time to go to college or be out on your own.

If you don't think you've had this kind of positive, major life change, know that you probably have. But if you can't think of one, imagine what it might be like to have everything transform so thoroughly that you know you can't ever go back to the way things were because you've moved from one phase of life to another very different and better one.

If you can recall such a time in your past, remember how you felt right before this life-changing event occurred. Maybe you had a sense of something on the way. Maybe not—maybe you were in despair and felt that life would never change, right before it did.

Recall that experience of life becoming so different that it marked a huge turning point in your personal history. It was the ending of a chapter and the beginning of a new one.

Look at your life now and imagine that everything to date has been moving you toward another major life change in the direction of your highest good. You don't necessarily see the details of what that change is, but imagine that you've received enough of a glimpse into your future to know that one is coming.

Spend today living with this knowing. Look around at the life you have with the perspective that there are things you'll soon be saying goodbye to, and things that will soon feel like part of a whole different lifetime. You may feel some sadness as you recognize that it's the end of the world as you know it, yet you sense the change will lead you somewhere your heart has always longed to be. Move around in your life with a growing sense of anticipation, knowing that something wonderful is about to happen!

And as you read these words and have your own small journey in consciousness, be aware of the many others who have or will encounter these words: the many minds stopping here for a moment, suspending disbelief, dreaming and wondering; hearts growing expectant... Imagine that you can sense the accumulation of anticipation that has collected around these words, just as you might get a "feeling" when you pause at a spot where many have stopped to reflect and wonder.

If you choose to keep reading, know that there are adventures ahead that may have already changed you. You don't need to believe this, just imagine how it would feel if you did...

And you will find us along the way—the many of us who, like you, have paused here for a moment and agreed to take this journey together.

Beyond time and space, we have already loved you and rooted for your success.

Welcome, dear friend! We have been waiting for you!

Chapter 2: The Seeds of Change—The Power of Us All Together

If you are old enough to remember the 1980s, you might recall that it was a time for glorifying the power of the individual. Iconic movie character Gordon Gekko, positively glamorous in his greedy exploitation, preached that greed is good; Madonna sang of being a "Material Girl"; New Age guru Louise Hay introduced us to the higher octave of personal power, teaching the importance of self-love and the power we each have to shape our own reality.

But in the midst of this "me" era, the seeds of Unity Consciousness were quietly being sown. An important spiritual event took place on August 17, 1987 in the form of the "Harmonic Convergence." On this date there was an unusual astrological alignment of planets and it was said to be the beginning of an ascension phase in humanity's evolution. It has been related to the start of a new phase of peace on earth and of moving out of three-dimensional reality into fourth-dimensional reality—in other words, out of the illusions of time, space and separateness, and into the reality of oneness and limitlessness.

Though I was aware of the Harmonic Convergence when it occurred, I gave it little attention. By 1987 I had been deeply involved in the study and teaching of metaphysics for more than a dozen years, but I've always tended to distance myself a bit from the subjectivity of spiritual events that are defined purely by their refined vibrations; vibrations that can only be felt and interpreted by an elite few. With tongue in cheek, I refer to this as the "High Woo" of spiritual thought and, consequently, let the Harmonic Convergence pass without actively participating—a little too "Woo" for my taste. I can't say that I've thought much about it since. Until, that is, as I prepared material for a new workshop in 2014.

There are times when I feel that something has just come to me or through me from some higher place. I feel certain that we all have this experience. My impulse to look at our times through the frame of the obscure, long ago event of the Harmonic Convergence and the related astrological markers was just such an experience. It didn't seem to come from me. I say this because, as I said, the Convergence didn't make a huge impression on me when it happened, and I hadn't thought of it in years.

But even more significantly—and this is a bit disconcerting to me—I have absolutely no recollection of the thought process that led me to think about the Harmonic Convergence and relate it to my work. I have asked myself time and again what inspired me to go back to that event, let alone track the Saturn cycles related to it, and I draw a complete blank. I have no memory whatsoever of this thought first occurring to me. In that my sensibilities judged it to be far too subjective for public presentation, I didn't at first expect it to be incorporated into a workshop, let alone become part of a book.

But once I started on the crazy rabbit chase of the Harmonic Convergence, the planet Saturn, and the unprecedented events of our times, I got chills and gooseflesh of the highest degree and couldn't turn back or keep it to myself. So I hope you will stay with me—even if this is going too deeply into the Woo weeds for your sensibilities—and draw your own conclusions.

The primary organizer of the world-wide events that took place on the day of the Harmonic Convergence was José Arguelles:

> *There comes a point when things have to change. A vibration signal was sent out. Where the signal was coming from—whether it was coming from our genetic coding, whether it was coming from the Earth, whether it was coming from outer space, or whether it was coming from all of those—this signal went out and people responded to a signal. It is very much like when a species gets a signal to change the direction of its migration pattern. The signal was, "Go back to the Earth ... if you want peace on this planet, go back to the Earth."*
>
> – José Arguelles on the Harmonic Convergence[1]

Arguelles believed that at the Harmonic Convergence point, the world would either begin a new phase of peace or be destroyed.

Whether or not you buy into the notion of a "vibrational signal," this event had cultural and historical significance in that it was only the second time consciousness had been organized on a massive, synchronized, global scale toward world peace, the first being the World Healing Meditation, initiated by John Randolph Price, held just months earlier on December 31, 1986. This latter event called for twenty million people to envision world peace at the same time to shift the collective consciousness on the planet. While there had been other huge events dedicated to raising funds and awareness for the common good, in these two events the currency was spiritual consciousness, using it as an agent of change.

Perhaps the only thing that compared to this wide-scale focusing of consciousness were the experiments introduced by the Transcendental Meditation organization headed by Maharishi Mahesh Yogi who, in 1960, predicted that if one percent of a population practiced TM, then the quality of life would improve for the whole surrounding community. Hundreds of experiments, conducted through the 1970s-90s, brought together groups of hundreds to thousands of TM practitioners and then studied changes in crime and other factors in the surrounding area. Many of these studies, showing highly significant improvements, sufficiently met scientific criteria to be published in a number of peer-reviewed scientific journals. Aside from being less massively scaled than these back-to-back world peace events in 1986-1987, the TM experiments were also different in that the meditation emphasized changing one's own attention rather than focusing intention on changing the world. Even when practiced in groups, these TM experiments seem to be more about amassing groups of solitary practitioners while the Harmonic Convergence events were a celebration of community.

The Harmonic Convergence lasted for three days, culminating on August 17, and drew people to hundreds of sacred sites all over the world for prayer, meditation, and ceremonies, with the clear intention of welcoming in a new world order.

Many famous people participated, including John Denver, Shirley MacLaine and Timothy Leary. Even Johnny Carson of *The Tonight Show* got his audience to chant "Om" for the event. Probably millions were touched in some way and nothing like it had ever happened before. Remember, at that time we weren't all connected by social media and the internet. It was a much bigger deal to organize something like this.

But how was this event anything more than a spiritual flash in the pan? Decades later, there's not much peace on earth to be found. Is there any evidence that the seeds of unity sown in 1987 have infiltrated culture in any significant way?

As this event was based on an astrological configuration, I explored this question for myself by looking at the planetary movements related to this auspicious date. In particular, I looked at the movement of the planet Saturn because, astrologically, Saturn is said to create time frames, stress points and structure.

A human life, an organization, or the birth of a spiritual impulse have something in common: they will be tested or go through a significant transition approximately every seven years. Astrological wisdom relates these seven-year cycles to the planet Saturn. Saturn, the seventh planet from the sun, takes approximately four seven-year cycles to travel 360 degrees, full circle, around the zodiac. The beginning of anything that has a clear starting date, be it something as tangible as a human life or as intangible as a marriage or organization with a precise incorporation date, will experience these testing points every seven years.

Rudolph Steiner, the creator of the "Waldorf" school movement, one of the largest independent school movements in the world, built this power of seven into the Waldorf curriculum, asserting that important developmental changes happen with each seven years of a human's life.

The expression "seven-year itch" comes from the idea that marriages begin to decline in happiness after seven years. Astrology suggests that these seven-year points test the strength of a person or entity, so that what is strong will solidify and what is weak will be stressed, sometimes to the point of breakdown.

If you look at your own life this way, not just by counting seven years but by actually looking at an ephemeris (a table charting the movement of planets by precise degree) to see exactly when Saturn has transited precisely 90 degrees, give or take a degree, around the zodiac from its position at your birth (or 180 degrees, 270 degrees, and so on), you may well find important events, periods of high stress, and turning points happening at roughly the seven-year point, the fourteen-year point, the twenty-one to twenty-two-year point, the twenty-eight to thirty-year point, etc.

I wondered: if a spiritual impulse was implanted in our collective consciousness on a specific date, signaling a new phase of human evolution, wouldn't there be similar phases of growth and testing at the seven-year points? Would it tell a story of humanity making an evolutionary leap?

In fact, when I looked at the Harmonic Convergence from this perspective, distinct phases of development became apparent with highly significant, global landmark events clustering around the seven-year stress points. (see the timeline on this in Appendix I.) What I will explore here in greater depth is how with each new phase of development toward unification and evolution, there were also growing challenges from an old order struggling to maintain dominance. These challenges both threatened Unity *and* urged it toward greater strength and manifestation, leading up to the greatest testing of all in 2016.

Treating the Harmonic Convergence as a birth and following its "growing up" in this way offers a compelling context for understanding the chaos of our times, for feeling hopeful, and for seeing what we need to do to move forward. Even if you doubt the validity of astrological influence, I hope you'll stay with me because what happened at the precise 90-degree stress points tells a powerful story.

According to this premise, the story begins with the "birth" of a new evolutionary journey in 1987, in a weekend culminating on August 17. Clustered around this event within the same year were two other significant consciousness events, one being the aforementioned World Healing Meditation. Another event that had some resonance with this new vibration to unify was held in October 1986 when Pope John Paul II organized the first World Day of Prayer in Assisi, Italy. He called together an assembly of 160 Christian and non-Christian religious leaders to spend the day together praying for peace. While it didn't quite capture the new evolutionary energy, which is characterized by egalitarian inclusiveness rather than an elite group of leaders, nothing like this had ever occurred before and it is interestingly clustered near in time to the next two, first-ever global consciousness events. If a vibrational signal truly was coming to change the direction of humanity, perhaps these first two events helped prepare the ground in some way.

The Astrological Symbolism of the Planet Saturn

Saturn rules structure, the skeletal system and all things hard and rigid. At its best, its influence is to give support, protection and necessary infrastructure. At its worst, it leads to inflexibility that breaks rather than bends with change.

Saturn rules time and old age. At its best, Saturn's influence confers wisdom and maturity. At its worst, it represents all that is old, devoid of life and needing to die in order to make room for something new to be born. The tests of Saturn often bring a feeling of time running out.

Saturn rules the power of authority which at its best becomes strong leadership and at its worst, authoritarian domination.

Saturn rules obstacles, limitations, trials and burdens. Ideally, this influence pushes us to find our strength, wisdom and resolve. At its worst, it breaks us down to our basest qualities of fear, small-mindedness and cruelty.

Jumping forward in time, tracking precise 90-degree intervals of Saturn's movement, I found a highly significant event at the half-way, 180-degree point in Saturn's journey around the zodiac. The date was September 11, 2001, the day the Towers fell in New York City—an event that left the world shaken. Another 90-degree progression further, landed in late September of 2008—the time when Lehman Brothers collapsed, starting the serious nose dive of the global economy that became known as the Great Recession.

The catastrophic nature of these events certainly speaks to Saturn's capacity to create stress and breakdown. In astrological symbolism, Saturn rules the end phase of a growth process: what was once vital becomes rigid, inflexible, outmoded and, consequently, vulnerable to stress, in the same way a dead tree becomes brittle and, in spite of—even because of—its size, can be easily blown down. This phase of dying from within and ultimate collapse is essential if anything new is ever to grow.

The escalating catastrophes of our times may well be showing us the dangerous remnants of a dying age—those things we must willingly release if we don't want them crashing down on us, much like the old dead tree in the yard that should have been taken down and is now lying buried in the roof after a big storm.

But the testing points of Saturn don't just create breakdown, they offer choices. These times provide opportunities to become greater by responding to stress in the highest way or to sink lower by succumbing to our basest impulses. The latter invariably leads to more breakdown, especially come the next seven-year testing point.

Immediately following 9/11, there was a brief time of people coming together, as so often happens following a crisis. The raw aftermath brought out the best in many of us. There was a spirit of solidarity and human kindness among usually divided Americans and much of the world stood with the United States. At this pivotal moment—Saturn's testing point—we had an opportunity to catch the wave of unity and join with the world to bring a criminal to justice. Instead, we waged war on the vast, unquantifiable vagaries of Terror, which has proven to be as effective as waging war against the boogeyman. The result has been the escalating breakdown of endless, unwinnable war. Osama bin Laden, the criminal mastermind of the 9/11 terror attacks, by his own admission set out to devastate America economically. He betted that U.S. leaders would spend unlimited funds trying to defeat him, and we've spent trillions.

As for the economic crashes and declines of the last several decades—most notably dramatic at Saturn's stress points—these have been the result of greed-driven practices amplified by the increasingly interconnected financial markets of the world, powerfully demonstrating the unsustainability of such practices in a world coming together.

1987, in fact, saw just such a clash between old-era greed and new order interconnectedness as the stock market went from an all-time high in August around the time of the Harmonic Convergence, to the historic crash of Black Monday a few months later[2]. This high-to-low was a result of the highly predatory trend in business that came about in the eighties. The still very new concept of "globalization" was driven home by the events of Black Monday, demonstrating how intertwined the global economy had become. Thomas Thrall, a senior professional at the Federal Reserve Bank of Chicago, described the dawning awareness and horror this crisis inspired in the financial community: "It felt really scary. People started to understand the interconnectedness of markets around the globe."[3]

These practices were inspired by a most extreme version of social Darwinism that began to influence world economics and policies in the 1980s. In the U.S., many in the Reagan administration embraced the philosophy of Ayn Rand. Author of such books as *The Virtue of Selfishness,* she was called the Reagan administration's "novelist laureate" in 1987 by the New York Times[4]. Rand has continued to be a guiding force for many Republican lawmakers, infusing American culture with the idea that selfishness and achieving wealth are morally good while altruism and poverty are morally bad. One of Rand's closest disciples was Alan Greenspan who was highly influential on the world's financial system as chairman of the Federal Reserve between 1987 and 2006 and has been credited with having a significant hand in engineering the economic crash of 2008.

The each-for-himself policies inspired by this extreme philosophy were not a purely American phenomenon. They blended seamlessly with those of then U.K. prime minister, Margaret Thatcher. Designed to give responsibility back to the individual to determine his or her own destiny, her policies eroded U.K. safety nets, weakened labor unions, shifted the tax burden from the rich to the poor, and infused Europe with an ideology of austerity and nationalism still playing out in 2016.

But amidst all the evidence of breakdown and unity challenged, does this tracking of Saturn give any glimpse of new growth, any sign of the new consciousness that supposedly was planted in 1987? And what happened at the first seven-year-stress point of Saturn in 1995?

1995 didn't have such direly evident events as 2001 and 2008. Again, this would seem to be in keeping with astrological wisdom which suggests the longer a planet lingers over a particular degree, the more powerfully visible its effects will be. This variance has to do with periods of a planet's retrograde motion where it will, from the earth's perspective, appear to pass over a degree, retrograde backward, hitting the same degree again, then go forward, making a third pass over the same point. The three transits of Saturn in 1987, 2001, and 2008, involved this kind of extended pass over and lasted for most of a year. But in 1995, Saturn made a very short, quick pass lasting just a few weeks, which might suggest a less visibly eventful development related to the progress of this unity impulse seeded in 1987.

There was, in fact, a highly significant event that took place in 1995, though it didn't make a huge splash at the time, and there were even reputable journalists saying it would never amount to much[5]. The years between 1987 and 1995 quite precisely bracketed the incubation phase of a world-changing phenomenon. 1987 marked the first year that the internet had significantly more users than the tiny, elite group it had prior to this time, and 1995 is when the internet was privatized and really took off in a huge way. So 1987-1995 is the period of time when the internet as we know it was developed and launched for mass consumption.

1995: The Internet and Evolution

Since then, the internet has played a huge role in evolving global consciousness, and I would go so far as to say it is one of the most, if not *the* most, significant cornerstones of our evolution. It has given rise to new models of egalitarian power and given access to global interconnectedness to nearly everyone. This quietly growing infrastructure has so quickly become a daily necessity that it's easy to lose perspective of its magnitude. As old infrastructures based on greed, fear and hierarchical power escalate to extremes with dire consequences that could destroy us, this amazing new infrastructure has been growing into a web of life that just might save us.

Deeply intertwined with the development of the internet is the development of cell phone technology. Though it was still in its primitive form compared to modern-day smart phones, in 1995 Sprint launched a brand new text messaging service. Text messaging began slowly but, as we all know, soon caught fire. These personal communication devices that traveled with us, and eventually also connected us to the internet, created a level of connectivity that humanity has never known. What's more, because establishing cell phone service in an area is far cheaper and easier than the infrastructure required for land-lines, parts of the world that once had little phone service at all now see the majority of inhabitants owning cell phones. A United Nations study in 2013 found that out of seven billion people on the planet, six million have cell phones—more than have toilets.[6]

Greater minds than mine also recognized the importance of the internet to our evolution. In 1995, when the World Wide Web was still brand new, well-known chaos theorist and philosopher Ralph Abraham called the internet a miracle and saw it as the material manifestation of Teilhard de Chardin's theory of noogenesis.

Pierre Teilhard de Chardin, the French philosopher active through the first half of the twentieth century, believed that, as humanity stopped evolving physically by branching into other species, we started evolving in consciousness. He predicted that humanity would come together in sympathetic, unified consciousness where no one was excluded. As he put it, "…entry into the superhuman [is] not thrown open to a few of the privileged nor to one chosen people.… They will open only to an advance of all together."[7] Significantly, De Chardin not only imagined us as a species capable of achieving super humanity, he prophesized that our salvation would be an egalitarian kind of experience requiring that we all go "together."

Early on, Ralph Abraham prophetically foresaw the potential of the internet to take us higher: not just to help us become better humans, but as the miracle that could save us from the "death track" of environmental exploitation, overpopulation, intolerance and greed that he saw accelerating. As he put it in a 1995 lecture, "We never could have survived until now if there had been no miracles in the past… and I figured the Web was one."[8]

A particularly notable effect of the internet is that it has birthed a whole millennial generation that has been profoundly shaped by a high level of connectivity and its easy access to decentralized, nonhierarchical, global communities. For the first time, a generation of tech-savvy young people are growing up to have more in common with their peers in other parts of the world than they do with older generations of their own culture. The young people born and maturing in this time frame since 1987 are showing an enormous proclivity for embracing principles of sharing, collaboration and egalitarianism, and are much less concerned about such differences as race, culture, sexual orientation or gender identity. Unlike the 1980s, when young urban professionals (dubbed "yuppies") aspired to heights of conspicuous consumption, today's youth aspire toward collaborative consumption, sharing economy, and sustainability—much of which is internet-enabled.

And everyday life as we know it is changing. Private bloggers are beginning to upstage corporate media, disseminating information unbound from the interests and money of big corporations; people are able to build careers through social media without the intermediary help of established industries; internet-enabled resource-sharing has become an important new business model (think Zipcar, Uber and Airbnb, for just a few well-known examples). Entrepreneur and best-selling author, Lisa Gansky describes in her book, *The Mesh—Why the Future of Business Is Sharing*,[9] how cooperative resource-sharing has become *the* hot new business model. Crowdsourcing has become an accessible, egalitarian means of generating resources by appealing to a large online community for small contributions in lieu of a single benefactor. In short, the internet has enabled a myriad of new "horizontal" (egalitarian, community based) forms of empowerment that are eclipsing old-style, "vertical" (hierarchical, from the top down) power structures. This is enabling a whole different model for personal success. Instead of "climbing the ladder of success," to use an old-model metaphor for hierarchical achievement, we're now learning how to create synergistic, egalitarian communities that empower everyone together.

2011 saw such a prevalence of egalitarian grassroots movements, facilitated by the easy connection of social media and cell phones, that Time Magazine acknowledged the trend by naming "The Protestor" their

2011 Person of the Year. They wrote, *"Almost all the protests this year began as independent affairs, without much encouragement from or endorsement by existing political parties or opposition bigwigs."*[10] Some of these organized protests even succeeded in bringing down governments.

Egalitarian movements, all internet assisted, have continued to gain momentum. As of 2016, the United States had seen the Occupy Movement, the Workers Movement, the Dreamers Movement, the Black Lives Matter Movement, the political "revolution" called for by Bernie Sanders, and the Standing Rock Sioux Water Protectors movement to block the Dakota Access Pipeline.*[1]

These many trends toward cooperation are enabled by the internet and forced into necessity by the catastrophic end results of greed, fear and hierarchical power. So, we see how the events of these Saturn stress points weave together, creating the crises that necessitate drastic change which, in turn, have propelled forward many new models for joining together. As developmental biologist Bruce Lipton puts it in his book, *Spontaneous Evolution,* "Crisis ignites evolution. The challenges and crises we face today are actually signs that spontaneous change is imminent. We are about to face our evolution."[12]

---

*The Tea Party Movement might seem like an omission here. I didn't include it simply for the reason that it had a great deal of financial backing from billionaires Rupert Murdoch and David and Charles Koch so doesn't fit the model of a purely grassroots movement.[11]

The Impact of the Internet

- It has given people all over the globe easy access to a huge wealth of information.

- The combination of internet and cell phone technology has connected people all over the world to information and each other, even people who once didn't even have access to phone service.

- It has given rise to social media and unprecedented forms of collective intelligence.

- It has profoundly shaped a whole generation to take global connectivity for granted.

- It has given rise to a wealth of new sharing economies both in personal and business spheres.

- It is diminishing our reliance on established industries and communication platforms by providing a means for accessing the public directly without an intermediary.

- It has enabled grassroots movements to organize and mobilize with a speed never before possible.

Exercise: Write Your Own Evolution Story

1. Identify the most significant challenges and crises that you currently experience in your life. If you come up with a long grocery list, see if one or two stand out as most influential.

2. Create a story of your life from the perspective that each one of these challenges and crises, be they clearly of your own making or circumstances that just seemed to happen to you, came to you purposely to fuel the next phase of your evolution. Imagine that each obstacle is pushing you to become something greater than you have ever been and write the story of how this progression has unfolded and continues to unfold into your future. You don't need to believe this to be true. Use your imagination and write a story about your path through challenge and what lies beyond.

    In your story, answer these questions:
    *   What new strengths are you developing in the process?
    *   What new joys does this path of evolution hold?
    *   What new behaviors does this path require?
    *   How does this path of evolution increase your positive impact on the world around you?

3. Spend a day living as if this story is true.

Chapter 3: The Point of Breakdown or Breakthrough

If you're like me and sometimes skip the introduction of a book in your impatience to get to the meat, let me repeat: 2016 was one game-changer of a year. There are many different stories about why this is coming from such diverse fields as economics, politics, and environmental science. But our story here is about an evolutionary impulse coming of age.

2016 was the year when Saturn came precisely full circle around the zodiac from where it was on the day of the Harmonic Convergence. This full, 360-degree circle from the birth moment of a life or entity is called the Saturn return, and is said to be a coming-of-age time when that which is weak falls apart, that which is strong becomes stronger, and there's an opportunity to see the consequences of our choices coming to fruition. In other words, it's the most severe testing point of the whole twenty-nine-year cycle where we reap what we have sown.

People often experience age twenty-nine to thirty as being a stressful and sometimes pivotal time of entering into the challenges of adulthood. If you are old enough to look back at this time in your life, you may recall it as a significant time of taking on new responsibilities and/or stresses associated with being an adult. Saturn being the astrological ruler of time itself, a Saturn return often brings a sense of time running out. Though some break down under the stress, others step up to new responsibilities and competencies.

How might this translate to the "growing up" of an evolutionary impulse? My own sense of it is that we have reached the "breakdown or breakthrough" point for humanity, both collectively and individually, where the extremes of all that's breaking down coexist in sharp contrast with quantum leaps forward into a new evolutionary phase.

In keeping with the Saturnian theme of time running out, by 2016 many earth scientists warned that dire environmental consequences are imminent if immediate action isn't taken. Some said it's already too late. The U.S., with its ultra-large carbon footprint, still had a significant segment of the population not believing climate change to be real, let alone a problem. And it was the only developed country with a major political party officially denying the reality of climate change, a party doing everything possible to slow or halt needed environmental protection actions. A Global Trends report released in 2014 by the U.K.-based marketing firm Ipsos MORI, identified the United States, the U.K. and Australia as being the three worst countries with regard to climate change denial.[1]

These three countries shared a common thread: Rupert Murdoch, the media mogul and himself a climate skeptic, who, as of 2016, controlled major media outlets in all three countries, including the staunchly climate change denying Fox News.[2]

This climate denying trend reflects any number of choices we collectively made over the previous few decades that could lead to even greater environmental breakdowns than the unprecedented storms, droughts, floods and fires we've already seen. The mega-consolidation of media and its power to bring humanity to a breaking point is just one prominent example of hierarchical power structures reaching their destructive end-game, like a cancer finally destroying its host.

By 2016, a consequence we saw unfolding from a choice made at the 2001 test point—to wage war on terror—was the skyrocketing of terrorist attacks around the world. What's more, our efforts to "be safe" made air travel cumbersome with huge amounts of money directed toward security measures. In a 2007 interview, Bruce Schneier, well-known security expert and author of several book on security including, *Beyond Fear: Thinking Sensibly about Security in an Uncertain World,* calls this spending of billions on rather obscure dangers to be "the theatre of security,"[3] meaning that it doesn't really make us safer; it just gives us a short-lived illusion of safety, until the next disaster strikes.

And then there's the death toll. According to a 2015 report put out jointly by Physicians for Social Responsibility, Physicians for Global Survival, and the International Physicians for the Prevention of Nuclear War[4], a conservative estimate of the number of lives lost in Iraq, Afghanistan, and Pakistan alone since the onset war following September 11, 2001 is at least 1.3 million, and could be in excess of two million. With the Middle East deeply destabilized, as of the time of this writing, there is no end in sight. At the breakdown or breakthrough point in 2016, it's hard to see anything other than severe breakdown resulting from the catastrophic decisions following 9/11 to live in fear and defend against all those who frighten us.

At a more localized level in the United States, this urgency to cling to the right to defend ourselves with the force of weaponry, has resulted in mass shootings becoming a daily occurrence, with the June 2016 shooting in Orlando's Pulse night club breaking the record as the biggest in modern U.S. history.

The greatest hope of the first few decades following the Harmonic Convergence might be the generation of people who've grown up in the time frame since 1987, with their easy acceptance of egalitarianism and sharing. They may just be the most obvious manifestation of the Harmonic Convergence unity impulse that's come to change the direction of our species. It's not surprising that these millennials fueled the unexpected rise of a most unlikely U.S. presidential candidate, Bernie

Sanders, who was too old, too unknown, too rumpled and grumpy, not to mention being a self-proclaimed socialist, to fit anyone's definition of a political superstar. But his egalitarian message, that by coming together we can take power back from the few and give it to the many, is one that powerfully spoke to the sensibilities of this generation.

The pivotal year of 2016, as the breakdowns and breakthroughs of the previous twenty-nine years all came to a climax, was certainly awash in extremes. The 2016 transit of Saturn made its touchdown in January (coinciding with a dramatic stock market drop) and the effects of the transit were felt throughout the year due to the slow and retrograding motion of the planet. It ended with one more exact pass over the precise degree in late October/early November of 2016, just as a new U.S. president was elected, suggesting that this election cycle is profoundly tied to the next twenty-nine-year phase of humanity's evolution.

With the sudden death of Supreme Court Justice Antonin Scalia in February shifting the conservative balance of the Court and the future of the U.S. Supreme Court up in the air, many political forecasters on both sides of the aisle were predicting that the 2016 election would determine the law of our land in enormously consequential ways for the next twenty-five to thirty years—which is the duration of the next, full-circle Saturn cycle of the Harmonic Convergence.

In 2016, the extremes of old and new played out powerfully on the political stage of the United States presidential election. The New York Times called the 2016 Republican platform the "most extreme Republican platform in memory,"[5] aiming to turn back the clock on a wide range of issues, while the Democratic platform, according to the Washington Post, was the most progressive ever[6].

Bernie Sanders did what no one imagined he could do: a virtual unknown with a near black-out of media coverage for the early months of his campaign and even some sabotage by the Democratic Party, he still came close to winning the Democratic nomination from political powerhouse Hilary Clinton. More amazingly, he did it with no super PAC money, relying instead on small donations from masses of people—proving what most savvy politicians believed to be impossible in this era of big money in politics, that votes could be won with the right message alone.

In that his message and campaign so closely followed the new, trending model that draws strength from the ground up rather than the top down, it's no wonder he captured the passion of millennials. He spoke to something that had already collectively shifted within us—especially for younger people. Sanders invited us to tap a power source that we've already begun to take for granted in other contexts: the power of all of us together.

In spite of not winning the nomination, he was still able to wield enough power to push Hillary Clinton's policies to the egalitarian left and was given power unprecedented for a losing candidate to help shape the 2016 Democratic platform into the progressive one it was. By May, Clinton had aligned herself with this new energy, changing campaign slogans from "I'm with her," to "Stronger together."

As new technology and a millennial generation give ever-growing momentum to a new era of global egalitarianism, the old order, represented by the most socially conservative and wealthy kingpins of mainstream hierarchical power (populated primarily by older, white males), has pushed harder than ever to maintain control. As surprising as Bernie Sanders' rise was, perhaps what many found even more astonishing was Donald Trump emerging as the Republican presidential candidate.

But maybe the assent of Donald Trump is not so surprising in this pivotal year of breakdown or breakthrough. As such a pure representation of old-paradigm hierarchical power, many who felt buffeted by the pressures of all that's breaking down embraced him with as much passion as millennials embraced Bernie Sanders. This group, most notably older, white, working-class people, looked to him to recover an eroding sense of security and power.

Trump came on the scene claiming, as did Sanders, not to be bought—but for the opposite reason to Sanders, because he claimed he could fund himself. He set himself outside of the vertical power hierarchy by virtue of being at the very top of it. With such a foothold in power, his rise was characterized by a freedom to do whatever he wanted—things that would ruin another politician's career. He even bragged that he could stand in the middle of 5th Avenue and shoot somebody and still not lose voters. [7]

While some wondered how the phenomenon of Trump could happen, viewed from the perspective of the white working class who have, more than most, felt their secure place in the world slipping away, Trump offered a heady taste of rebellious freedom ("I don't have to be politically correct if I don't want to!") and the reassurance that someone at the top would fix life to be more as it once was. A 2015 study showed a steep rise in the death rate of less-educated, 45-54 year old, white working class people with no other groups in the U.S. as affected, and no similar declines seen in other rich countries.[8] It correlates with a rise in suicide and addiction issues among this group, with increasing financial stress and dimming future prospects being suspected as the underlying cause.[9] By targeting such groups as Muslims, Mexicans, and all people of color, Trump gave his followers some sense of being higher up on the hierarchical chain of power by keeping others lower down.

Having a focus for anger and blame is one way to ameliorate a growing sense of feeling out of control and, consequently, hate crimes were on the rise. According to the Southern Poverty Law Center, the best-known resource for the reporting of hate crimes in the U.S., 2015 saw a sharp rise in hate groups and they cited Trump as part of the reason[10]. In another report based on a survey, they noted "an increase in bullying, harassment and intimidation" in schools as a result of students being "emboldened by the divisive, often juvenile rhetoric in the [presidential] campaign."[11]

What's more, as the world's weather has been doing scary, horrible things we've never seen before, it's understandable that many would find comfort in a political ideology that called climate change unreal and that promised to take us back to simpler times when everyone knew their place in a hierarchical social structure without such a push to have all ethnicities, genders and sexual orientations mingling on the same horizontal playing field.

Hillary Clinton won the popular vote by nearly three million and Bernie Sanders went on to create a new organization, "Our Revolution," to rally people toward greater involvement in social change. But Donald Trump won the presidential election.

The election proved to be a perfect storm that combined an antiquated electoral college system giving some states more voting weight than others, leaked emails that eroded Hillary Clinton's already lukewarm appeal, heavily-weighted media coverage, and massive voter suppression. Voter suppression efforts included such things as new restrictive ID requirements in Republican-dominated states (that particularly burdened the youngest, oldest and poorest voters), fewer voting sites in urban, democratic areas that forced people to wait for hours in line, and the Republican Interstate Voter Registration Crosscheck Operation.[12] This latter was a Republican operative that threw masses of voters off voting rolls in more than two dozen Republican-dominated states, often for simply having the same first and last name (with minorities being overly represented on these lists). The media played a significant role in the election as well, giving the outrageous reality star, Donald Trump, unlimited free air time. As the CEO of CBS said of Trump's presidential run at a conference in February of 2016, "It may not be good for America, but it's damn good for CBS... The money's rolling in and this is fun... Sorry. It's a terrible thing to say. But, bring it on, Donald."[13]

Of course, what enabled these various hijinks to succeed were the many, many eligible voters who simply chose to sit this election out. With the lowest turnout for a presidential election in twenty years, we collectively "chose" to elect as president a man who doesn't reflect the sensibilities of most of us and who, perhaps better than any other leader the U.S. has seen, personifies the end results of old-paradigm hierarchical power and the darkest aspects of our collective psyche.

Everything in this pivotal year took politics as usual into the realm of the unprecedented. From Sanders' phenomenal rise with no super Pac backing, to Clinton nearly becoming the first woman president, to Donald Trump defying all the rules and norms of politics, what unfolded seemed to take on mythic proportions and, regardless of what side you were on, the players became our superheroes and uber-villains.

But then, with the spiritual energies of evolution at work, perhaps there could be no "normal" in 2016. The forces that promised an inclusive, egalitarian future of wellbeing were locked in a titanic clash with the hierarchical powers of old that rule by fear, promising to keep us safe from the "other." Love and fear dueled to see which would predominate through the next twenty-nine-year cycle, and with so much on the line regarding humanity's long-term survival, the stakes had never been higher. It's no wonder that the politicians who emerged stepped into these larger-than-life energies and became the archetypes of our times.

I believe these unprecedented extremes are all signs that we have crossed a threshold of some sort. In the buildup to 2016, many others felt that something monumental was coming. Many climate scientists warned that we're near (or past) the tipping point of catastrophic climate change. Many economists predicted an extreme global economic crash around 2016—bigger than in 2008. Historian and political commentator, Thom Hartmann, wrote a highly insightful book, *The Crash of 2016,* meticulously putting together the history and the many reasons why this kind of crash is possible. In 2002, Robert Kiyosaki, financial commentator and author of the best-selling book, *Rich Dad, Poor Dad,* predicted that 2016 would see the worst stock market crash in history and in 2016 he still saw his prediction to be right on track[14].

But 2016, that began with a stock market crash, actually ended with an all-time stock market high. Each of the other extended passes of Saturn over the crucial 90-degree points—in 1987, 2001, and 2008 also included record stock market highs and/or lows. 2001 and 2008 included recessions. By early 2017, there were many reasons to believe that the 2016 high has some highly precarious underpinnings, not the least of which is the Chinese economy facing a massively growing debt crisis[15] that could ripple through the global economy.

Billionaire Warren Buffet spoke frankly to the financial unpredictability of the times in his 2016 letter to shareholders of his multinational conglomerate, Berkshire Hathaway, citing the ever-growing possibilities of cyber, biological, nuclear or chemical attack on the United States as well as the unknowns of climate change posing an unavoidable risk to American corporations.[16] By early 2017, the presidency of Donald Trump threatened to make all of these factors increasingly volatile with his climate change-denying cabinet intent on rolling back environmental regulations and his undisciplined approach to international affairs.

Spiritually, as 2016 neared, some Christian groups saw an unusual supermoon lunar eclipse that took place on September 27, 2015 as heralding the beginning of the long-prophesized end times—a time of tribulation before redemption, while metaphysical seers interpreted the same event to mean that we've reached a powerful turning point in humanity's evolution, a tipping point in consciousness where there are now enough of us aligned with a high vibration of love to tip the planet in a new, better direction.

In these fantastically extreme times that begin the second twenty-nine-year maturing cycle of the Harmonic Convergence, and perhaps the most important twenty-nine years in humanity's destiny, there seems to be little option other than to break down or break through.

But where do the next Saturn stress points fall in the second twenty-nine-year cycle and what can we expect?

I have deliberately left these dates out of this writing because I don't want to create in any of us a sense of anticipatory dread that we give energy toward fulfilling. The future—as well as the past—is what we are here to create. As we will explore in greater depth later, the power of conscious intention is so vast, mysterious and limitless that it is capable of flowing through not only space, but through time as well. Yes, consciousness can even change the past.

Certainly those things that are recorded in history may not bend easily through our intent, but who knows how many seeds have been planted (or could be planted retroactively) that have invisible tendrils waiting to burst into manifestation at some pivotal time? As a playful venture into creating our future, let's first give attention to the past; not the recorded history that we have reviewed here, but to the seeds of possibility that were planted long ago, awaiting the right moment to sprout.

Exercise: Sowing the Seeds of Change

Quiet your mind for a moment and let your attention float free. Take a deep breath or two to help you transition to a soft, open mental state...

Go back in your mind to 1987 (no matter if you weren't born yet, your consciousness existed) and imagine yourself scattering seeds of love over the planet. See them rooting in the earth, shining as stars overhead, landing in the hearts of millions.

There are many of us doing this together and it's not hard or serious work. Have a light and gentle daydream of this. Let it bring a smile to your face. Some of these seeds land in your own heart and in your own personal history, ready to sprout the moment you're ready for them. Don't try to understand what this means, just enjoy knowing they're there.

Now do the same over the time frame of 1995. Shower seeds everywhere... Shine love through all the connections of the burgeoning internet... Let it be a fun and playful activity...

Move on to 2001. As the world appears to darken, scatter a barrage of light-filled seeds of hope, healing, and love. You don't need to understand any of this. You don't even need to believe that it's doing anything. As we will explore later, it's not necessary to believe in order for your intention to have a powerful effect. Just imagine how it would feel if you did believe that your thoughts, along with those of other readers, are making the world a radically better place.

Now move your mind to 2008. Rejoice as you see some of the seeds of unity that you planted in the earlier times manifesting, bringing us together in amazing new ways of sharing. Spread masses of new seeds all through this time period. See them as having the potential to heal scarcity as we've known it and help us all to thrive. Feel a burst of delight as you do this...

Now drop clouds full of seeds into 2016. See them take root everywhere. See all of us who are reading these words, thousands of us, spreading so many seeds that they create an interlocking root system under the earth and a unified net of energy through the atmosphere. See our seeds finding homes in so many hearts that we are joined together in an indivisible web of love all over the globe. No one is left out of this web, even those who try to exclude themselves. Can you picture all of these seeds bursting into bloom?

Chapter 4: Breaking Through to Leadership

The breakdown or breakthrough point is where life takes a radical turn for the better because we choose to align ourselves with love instead of fear, or we experience increasing crises because we fearfully try to hold on to what has been—which in these times is no longer an option. We choose the path of breakthrough by taking bold action in the direction of what we know is right even if it takes us out of our comfort zone. We attend to what we know is important without putting it off any longer. We listen to inner guidance and believe what we know in our hearts even if we don't have physical evidence of a predictable outcome. The exercise in this chapter offers an opportunity to put all of these principles into practice.

Alternately, if we let fear, apathy, ambivalence, procrastination, denial, or unconsciousness determine our choices—or lack of them—we see our circumstances take a turn for the worse. Change *will* come—either swiftly as a great leap into higher levels of wellbeing, or more painfully through crises that forcibly clear away the old. Consequently, it's more important than ever to choose which path we are going to align ourselves with: the last wave of separateness, fear, and limitation, or the new one of unity and egalitarian wellbeing. If we're not aligning ourselves with the new paradigm of our times, we may well find ourselves getting bogged down in all that's falling away. The good news is that we each get to choose which way we go. Sacrificing our reliance on comfort and old patterns can drastically alleviate the need for struggle and can propel us into incredible breakthroughs.

The following are some of the major themes of our times that I believe will characterize the second twenty-nine years in the life of the Harmonic Convergence call to Unity, playing out in both global scenarios as well as in our individual personal lives. Consider the following and see if any of it feels familiar to you:

- Everything feels extreme and polarized duality is everywhere.
- Old forms of security are ripped away.
- Changes come about suddenly and surprisingly.
- Important decisions must be made or crisis will result.
- We are faced with the greatest challenges of our lives and/or finally feel free for the first time in a long time.
- Creativity and inspiration skyrocket.
- The breakthroughs we've been waiting for come about suddenly, even after we've given up hope.
- We feel responsible as never before for the well-being of humanity and the planet.
- Standing together brings power and ease.

Seizing the breakthroughs that are more available now than ever instead of waiting for life to act upon us requires that we become leaders, but not in the old-style, hierarchical, follow-me-and-do-as-I-say mode of leading.

New leadership operates in accordance with the new rules of quantum physics and is fractal rather than hierarchical. In a hierarchy, one leads through one's commands, but in a fractal paradigm, where every bit of the whole reflects all of the whole, it is only possible to lead with one's being. In quantum reality, any time a part of the whole changes, it affects all of the rest. Accordingly, as any one of us changes, we affect everything and everyone. New leadership is all about being so present, transparent, and willing to surrendering to God's agenda—which comes through our inner guidance, not necessarily our linear thinking—that others are changed and led by the power of our example.

So, what marks the difference between purely personal growth and this heightened state of new leadership? Purely personal growth may well be accomplished within the limited, Newtonian world view paradigm. From this perspective, we see ourselves as single entities that can be separated out from the rest, changing without it affecting the rest, and acted up by our environment in random ways we can't control. Within this world view we can certainly make many decisions that will enhance our well-being.

Alternately, in the paradigm of new leadership, we understand that we affect everyone and everything with our every thought and action. In this expanded world view, we recognize that "personal" growth ultimately leads us into greater responsibility for the world. Then our growth not only accomplishes something for ourselves, we create a far bigger ripple in the world.

A big difference between personal growth and new leadership is the consciousness with which it's done. The consciousness of leadership creates an expanded outcome where we find our own personal destiny increasingly encompassing the greater good of all. What's more, this is when we truly breakthrough to thriving, because to thrive in these times requires that we bring to life an agenda larger than simply getting what we want.

The exercise in this chapter is an opportunity to step into leadership in this way. In keeping with a quantum paradigm, it is inherently nonlinear and nonhierarchical. It involves listening to your inner guidance and, if so guided, stepping out in faith even though the whole path isn't visible and doesn't guarantee a comfortable or controllable outcome.

This exercise asks you to commit to an act of leadership without first knowing what the act is by trusting your inner guidance to direct you appropriately. As powerful as this kind of leap of faith is when the time for it is right, it's something that can't be forced, only inspired. Only you know when you're ready for such a step and it's important that you undertake this exercise only if you're guided from within rather than by the book.

Accepting the call to lead is a step into the unknown because when we truly follow this call, we find ourselves following Spirit's plan, not our own personal agendas. This path may well feel uncertain, unfamiliar and even out of our control, yet it ultimately takes us further than our smaller agendas ever could.

The exercise works on a synchronicity principle. Through synchronicity and inner guidance, you will receive a message. Synchronicity is a term psychologist Carl Jung gave to the law of meaningful coincidence where events that have no clear cause and effect relationship can nevertheless "coincidentally" have a profoundly meaningful connection. This principle is very in keeping with the new rules of the quantum world view even though it doesn't seem to make sense from the older, Newtonian paradigm.

Through synchronicity, the message that you randomly receive will be one that has personal relevance for you at this time. The use of randomness in this way is a powerful means for inviting higher wisdom and guidance to break through the barrier of our limited perspective. It has a way of introducing a wild card element, quickly taking us beyond what we already know to what we need to know.

The purpose of the message is to show you an aspect of new-paradigm power that you particularly need to develop in order to manifest your personal highest good. It is what will best help you move with the energy of breakthrough in your life rather than breakdown.

The message you receive may be something that you've been resisting. It may be outside of your comfort zone. Or, it might be just what you've been working on because you've already sensed its importance for you.

Before going into the exercise, reflect a moment on an area of your life that you deeply desire to see change. It might be an area of breakdown that you would like to see turn in a positive direction. It might be an area where you are ready to experience a quantum leap into a new level of success, fulfillment and wellbeing. It might even be something that feels impossible or far out of reach. Perhaps it's something that you have worked on changing or manifesting but haven't yet succeeded. Whatever you choose, limit it to a single focus rather than a grocery list of desires, and let it be something that you truly care about. When you have something in mind and you feel ready, continue on...

Exercise: New Leadership

Relax your body and quiet your thoughts with some deep, slow breaths. Bring to mind the change you so deeply desire. If it's something you have struggled with, in this moment, just hold it lightly. Let go of worries or problem-solving. Gently hold it in the light of possibility, without even quite knowing what this means... and then let it go, as easily as you would release a butterfly that came to sit on your hand.

In a little while, you will consult your inner guidance as to whether it's time for you to accept the opportunity in this exercise to be a leader. This is not a one-size-fits-all exercise and it's important to listen to your guidance around whether it's right for you.

Recognize that your inner Guide is purely benevolent and leads you only in the direction of your best interests. It isn't punishing; it has no agenda to push you beyond your limits or into harm. It simply sees the bigger picture of what is best for you in ways your conscious mind can't always see. Take a moment to make friends with this wise and loving place in yourself. Feel that it is trustworthy. If you don't believe you have this source of inner counsel, just imagine what it would feel like if you did... and say hello...

Should you be called to lead here, it means accepting an assignment before knowing what the assignment is. The exercise is structured this way because this is how life is. Inner guidance often urges us toward a step into the unknown without showing us the next five steps beyond, or even the next single step, and yet, when the urge is coming from within and not from external pressure, it's sure to lead us where we need to go.

To start feeling out your readiness, ask yourself: if having the change you deeply desire meant accepting in total faith and trust the action step Spirit puts before you, would you? If it meant stepping out of comfortable familiarity to do something challenging or unfamiliar, would you? If it meant loosening personal control enough to allow the hand of Spirit to lead the way, would you?

Understand, though, that breaking through into a new paradigm of wellbeing is never guaranteed to be a predictable journey. Sometimes the joy we've never known can be a far more frightening experience than the struggle and limitation that's familiar. The highest good that God has for us, the places our heart longs to go, may bear no resemblance to the limited agendas we've grown attached to over the years simply because we've lost our understanding of anything better. So, if do you choose to answer this call to leadership, get ready for an exciting ride that may unfold more quickly and differently than you expect!

If you don't feel ready for this level of unfolding, you can choose to let the energy of those who are take you where you need to go—and this is fine. This is part of the new energy of our times—things become easier when we do them together. The trick here is to really listen to your highest voice on this. If you're feeling called but choose not to step up due to fear or inertia, trying to hold on to the comfort of what's familiar, then you may be setting yourself up for breakdown.

On the other hand, if you are pushing yourself to step up simply because you feel you should, perhaps because you hold yourself up to harsh expectations of perfection, or because you rarely trust that you can rely on the energy of others, then you, too, may still be acting from old patterns of limitation rather than genuinely moving forward into breakthrough.

Whatever you choose authentically from within is the path of greatest growth for you so there is no push here to identify yourself as a leader if it isn't right, right now. What is most important is that if you do get the call to leadership, that you commit yourself to it whole-heartedly, and act upon it, even if it takes you into uncharted territory.

So truly listen to where the breakthrough lies for you. Let your inner guidance help you with this now. See if you are feeling called to take a bold step here into the unknown of new leadership without quite knowing what's to come, just trusting that your inner guidance won't steer you wrong. It doesn't matter whether you get an inner yes or inner no, so long as you are listening...

Now, regardless of your guidance, to lead or abstain, pick a number from one to twelve. You can't do this wrong so don't struggle with it.

⟐⟐⟐⟐⟐⟐⟐

Your number determines your message so refer to the chart at the back of the book in Appendix II. Look at the list of messages and find the one with the correlating number.

As you reflect on this message, give some thought as to how it may relate to your life right now and why synchronicity delivered this particular message to you instead of any of the others. Imagine that it is related to the change you most desire and listen to how your inner guidance may be using this message to keep you on course. If the message doesn't feel "right," don't be too quick to throw it away even though it doesn't immediately resonate. Keep it in mind for a few weeks and see if you begin to hear this same guidance from different sources in your life. When we need a message, Spirit will whisper it to us again and again until we are ready to listen.

If you were guided to step up into new leadership here and now there is, as promised, a special assignment for you to practice over the coming week. Your act of leadership is to seek out ways to work with your message in the highest, most authentic way you possibly can. Look for ways to be, to do and to receive this aspect of empowerment throughout the week. Look for ways to stretch beyond familiar, comfortable behavior as you do this so that you take the insight of this message and truly turn it into personal growth. And as you do this, hold in your consciousness an awareness of the many other readers working with this exercise. Imagine that you are doing this for all of us. Imagine that as you step into your highest self in this way, you create a vibration of transformation that serves all of us as it also directly benefits you.

If you did not feel called to take the leap of faith into leadership before reading into the exercise, and now wish you had, it's not too late. No, this isn't a suggestion to do the exercise over now that you know what it entails. We rarely get that choice in life. This is an opportunity to transform your choice into your own breakthrough by accepting a different assignment this week. Your assignment is to spend the week shining your love and gratitude to those who were clearly guided to lead. Especially hold in gratitude those who are working with the same message that you are. Imagine that you are able to send this loving intention across space and through time to everyone in the past, present, and even the future, who have, who are and who will practice this exercise. Have faith in them and trust that their work is furthering your growth.

Imagine that you are a miracle-maker, that your love is so powerful it can change someone's life for the better, and that you receive great joy from sharing your miraculous gift. You don't need to believe this about yourself, just imagine how it would feel if you did and act "as if." If you do this with as much whole-hearted sincerity as you can, it will give those who chose to lead the support they need to fulfill their assignment and to benefit all of us at the same time. Again, you don't need to believe this, just imagine.

Questions for Thought

- How have you let opportunities to embrace your destiny as a leader slip away in your life?
- How do you allow fear, passivity, and reluctance to stop you?
- What are you willing to do this week to step into new leadership?

Note: If you review this exercise at another time, you can build in the element of synchronicity and uncertainty by writing numbers 1-12 on 3x5 cards, shuffling and picking randomly from the deck to find your message.

Chapter 5: Time to Upgrade our Spiritual Practices

When I first encountered the ground-breaking work of Louise Hay and other mind-over-matter teachings in the early 1980s, it was galvanizing! Realizing that my thoughts create my reality rocked my world. I happily wrote pages and pages of affirmations and felt empowered in a way I hadn't before. When I felt at the mercy of my circumstances, I had tools to take back my power. And it worked... at least sometimes. It was also awakening to hear that it wasn't selfish to love myself and to want more from life. It was just what I needed.

But after several decades, these ideas no longer feel fresh. I frequently hear from dedicated law of attraction students who have made their vision boards, written affirmations, visualized, and have seen interesting synchronicities appear while the big issues continue to remain elusive. As one person asked me, "I've gotten all the little things on my vision board but how do I get the big stuff to manifest?" Many have become cynical. Perhaps what was fresh and exciting in the eighties simply hasn't grown with the times. Think of all that has changed since then: the internet, the economy, the environment... us.

The 1980s saw a whole genre of literature emerge, pioneered by people like Louise Hay, Shakti Gawain, and a number of others, who took older metaphysical teachings and blended them with modern psychology, making them into very accessible personal growth tools for healing and empowerment. This genre continued to grow in popularity for decades. These teachings place a lot of emphasis on self-love, on having it all, and on getting what we want. When they first came out they were new, exciting, and powerful. They fit with the times. The politics and the culture in the U.S. were all about the power of the individual to have, not just a good life, but to have it *all,* and to get it through cleverness rather than hard work. The "New Age" spiritual teachings of the era were similarly themed, teaching that our state of mind has unlimited power and anyone who can properly harness it can create fabulous results without hard work.

This was very different from the standard of mid-twentieth century decades which idealized an "American Dream" where anyone who worked hard enough on a linear trajectory could become part of a vast middle class. These times weren't so much about having it all as having enough for a materially secure life. Aspiring to become part of this middle class came with the expectation of hard work, pulling one's weight, and a requirement to conform to current social norms. Of course, this ideal only applied to the mainstream, white majority of the time.

The 1960s saw a wide scale rebellion against social norms and limitations to personal freedom. The civil rights movement challenged centuries of racial repression; the feminist movement challenged the restrictive roles ascribed to women; hippy culture challenged the emphasis on materialism and conformity of earlier decades. Through the seventies, conformity as a prerequisite for advancement was thrown out the window as we all set about "doing our own thing" (a term that started entering our vocabulary in the late sixties). By the eighties we were beginning to collectively assimilate some version of the idea that each of us created our own reality and that it was okay to want more from life.

Now well into the 21st century, it's easy to see that the 1980s "greed is good" impulse has gone too far: the crimes of Wall Street have wreaked havoc on the global economy and the crimes of industry have jeopardized the environment. But still, the essential lessons of the eighties were important: that consciousness is powerful and reality is fluid; that we don't need to conform to or be held back by the world around us; that self-love isn't selfish—it's necessary if we are to thrive, not just survive, and that it's okay to seek an abundant life.

As Bruce Lipton suggests, "crisis ignites evolution"; perhaps we needed greed to go to extremes, in order to come fully into this new era of cooperation. Because we are increasingly connected financially, environmentally, and technologically, for better or worse we simply can't separate ourselves anymore. Perhaps a blessing of the financial, political and environmental crises of our times is the way they are forcing us toward greater interdependence and toward placing value differently— less on possessions and more on love and connection. Cooperation, collaboration and community in a wide range of applications are coming into vogue not because they're morally better than purely personal advancement, but because they're a better path to it. We have been forced by crisis to find better options.

"Circular economy," "sharing economy," "collaborative consumption," "crowd-sourcing," and "open-sourcing" are just a few terms that have entered our vocabulary since the turn of the 21st century. All these refer to the sharing and disseminating of goods, services and information in a decentralized, peer-to-peer fashion enabled by the internet, without the involvement of a central authority. They require and encourage mass participation to drive them, they encourage the most efficient use of resources, and they minimize inequities of power and resources while they simultaneously empower individuals.

The New Operating Model

This is the emerging new order. It's one where
individuals are empowered beyond anything
we've previously known through small efforts
contributed by masses of us into an organizing
infrastructure. These contributions are most often
from unpaid volunteers. The process is win/win;
it's easy; it's the virtually limitless power of all
of us together sharing rather than taking. It lacks
the linear structure inherent in hierarchies,
having more similarity to the new quantum model
of indivisible energy.

Even if you haven't noticed, the new operating model is in play all
around us. When I first moved into my large, urban neighborhood ten
years ago, neighbors rarely reached out to each other. But now there is an
active sharing among neighbors of free or low-cost goods, services, news,
help, events and ideas via Nextdoor.com, a nation-wide social media
network connecting neighbors. A friend of mine went on vacation and
stayed in the charming guest suite of a private home through Airbnb
instead of booking the Marriot—getting more and paying less. The streets
of my city are peppered with tiny, rentable Smart Cars and rental bike
stations so that people no longer have to own their own vehicle and
compete for parking. Every time the smallest question runs through my
mind, I take out my phone and Google it. I have answers in seconds that,
twenty years ago, would have taken days of research, if I could find them
at all. These are all examples of individuals being empowered as never
before by masses of people making small contributions into an organizing
infrastructure. It's the power of getting more for less by sharing together

rather than taking for oneself.

But what does this have to do with spiritual practices? In spite of the rise of such a radically new paradigm trending in areas of science, technology, business, culture, and politics, much of what is still being written and taught in popular personal empowerment teachings is rooted in the wave of literature that came out in the eighties, teaching us the power we have to separate ourselves from the collective experience and to create our own reality. As important as these teachings were when they first came out, they don't fit with current times where the greater power lies in *having a collective experience* rather than separating from it.

Perhaps the best known work in the law of attraction genre is the book and movie, *The Secret,* which became a cultural phenomenon when it was featured on the Oprah Winfrey Show in 2006. In a way, it marked a perfect culmination to this wave of teachings. The enormous attention, both positive and negative, that law of attraction teachings received around this time, I believe, marked a point of collective assimilation of these essential ideas that had roots in the 1980s. In other words, their becoming part of mass culture signaled their expiration date. Not that they've suddenly become wrong, just that we have now evolved to a place where they are no longer enough. Even the title, "The Secret," and its implied meaning of knowledge accessible to only an elite few—as the arcane wisdom of metaphysics once was—speaks to an older era and not to the new reality of open-sourced knowledge accessible to all.

Interestingly, 2006 was about the same time that social media as we know it today was birthed. Twitter began in 2006 and the social media giant Facebook started just two years earlier in 2004, turning us into one big global community of "friends." The era of the collective had truly arrived but how is this showing up in our spiritual teachings? Locking ourselves away with our affirmation journals, vision boards, and personal success visualizations, intent on getting what we want, is a very singular, separating experience and this just doesn't reflect who we collectively are anymore. It doesn't address the deeper evolutionary needs of humanity to come together. Even more importantly, as we're discovering in so many contexts, the pure pursuit of our own personal gain is no longer the most effective path to personal fulfillment.

Law of attraction teachings tell us to focus on what we want, create the vibration of it within ourselves and then it will show up. Hypothetically, this is valid—if we can really stay in the vibration of what we love, because love in any of its many forms is highly magnetic. But this light, expansive state of mind can be difficult to hold. What begins as a delightful feeling of, "wouldn't it be wonderful!" can so easily devolve into an obsessive state of attachment. We start watching and waiting for signs of what we want to show up; we wonder if it will ever show up; we worry that it won't. All of a sudden, instead of living in the moment in an expansive state of joy, we're contracting into worry about a future outcome. We become caught up in our own insular, little world, which isn't an effective state for attracting our desires.

Evolving metaphysical practices in alignment with the new operating model that is trending in other contexts would somehow need to introduce an element of mass participation into the process of calling forth our own desires. Since those first mass consciousness events, in 1986 and 1987, there have been many such events organized for world peace and wellbeing. But this doesn't quite fit the model of an easy infrastructure with immediate access that benefits the individual as it serves the whole.

In my book, *Holding a Butterfly*, I introduced a kind of infrastructure for consciousness by inviting every reader to join in loving intention with every other reader to create an energy field that would raise everyone higher. Simply reading the book and practicing the exercises with intent brought small donations of many individuals' loving consciousness together into a collective pool.

As outlandish as this sounds, I included along with the exercises some of the amazing new science of consciousness documenting what research is showing us about the incredible power of consciousness to join across space and time, to amplify, to heal, to affect physical reality, and to even affect physical events in the past. New science is suggesting that the Zero Point Field, which essentially is a limitless energy field underpinning all existence, is the true repository of memory and information, and not the brain. The brain acts more like an individual computer accessing information from a collective, external pool. The modern computer connected to the World Wide Web is a fairly good model for the less tangible but no less real workings of consciousness. Organizing infrastructures such as Google, Wikipedia, and Facebook are driven by small contributions from masses of individuals and bring easy access to countless resources. So why not do the same thing with consciousness? Clearly, the internet is playing a huge role in evolving humanity. It may well be giving us the blueprint for what can be done with consciousness alone.

Over the years since *Holding a Butterfly* was published, I have expanded the infrastructure introduced in the book through my live and recorded presentations, identifying many related exercises in consciousness as "miracle experiments," inviting participants to imagine joining in loving consciousness with every other miracle experiment participant to access the combined energy of all of us. The simple intention put around these miracle experiments—the intention to join in love with *everyone* who ever has or ever will participate in any of these exercises identified as miracles experiments—creates the infrastructure that pools our individual contributions. Why would this work? It works simply because we are imaginative enough to envision it, and because we want it with heartfelt intent. According to what research is showing us about the far-reaching capabilities of intention, this is enough.

To illustrate how this works, here's a brief exercise:

Bring to mind your highest heart's desire—just as law of attraction teachings would suggest. Imagine it vividly for a moment, as though it's already come to pass. Let the imagining fill you with pleasure... and then let it go. This is where popular practices end and the new model begins.

Now, imagine yourself able to reach out, beyond time and space, to every other person who has, is, and will ever read these words (you don't have to believe this to be possible, just imagine what it would feel like if you did). Imagine that we're all joining minds, bringing only our highest and best to the meeting, forming a pool of consciousness (what biochemist Rupert Sheldrake might call a morphic field).

To activate this field of consciousness, for a moment, let yourself love all of these unseen, unknown, fellow participants. Not for any reason, just because you can. Love them with all your heart as you would your nearest and dearest.

Let their hearts' desires matter to you as much as your own and, with the biggest wave of love you can muster, send (in your imagination) the heartfelt desire that miracles now happen for each and every one of them. Imagine yourself as a parent delivering the most beautifully wrapped birthday gift to your beloved child (multiplied many times), with your heart overflowing from the sheer joy of giving the perfect gift. You don't need to believe this is really doing anything. Just imagine how it would feel if you did believe that your loving intention is quietly making life better for people you'll never know. Imagine how overjoyed these recipients feel to experience a great blessing coming their way...

There. You've done it. And now countless people you'll never meet have just done the same for you. Didn't it feel pretty good to want the best for all those unknown people? And doesn't it feel good knowing they're all on board, making miracles happen in your life? In the artful mastery of the power of intention, all of these "good" feelings are creative acts that attract wellbeing into your life in all kinds of mysterious ways.

They also turn you into a miracle worker touching the lives of many in ways possibly more profound that you will ever know.

If given full attention, that exercise could be an effective practice for calling forth *your* heart's desire, yet most of it is spent being in service to countless others, people you'll never meet. Many readers of *Holding a Butterfly* have reported stories of miraculous healings and manifestations related to reading the book. But what I find even more significant is how many speak of feeling less alone, more loved, more compassionate and more "connected."

As energy healers, prayer practitioners and researchers into consciousness know, holding a loving intention to help another person has a positive effect on both the giver and the receiver. When a whole group does this for one another, it has an exponential effect. We raise each other up in a way that enables us all to attract our highest good with greater ease. This is when we attract miracles—things far better than anything we had envisioned.

Another thing that this element of joining does is that it helps keep us from going into a counterproductive place of worry and attachment. When we feel love around our own heart's desire, and then shift attention to loving someone else and feeling joyful about their highest good, we're less likely to start obsessing about ourselves. We remain in a state that traditional law of attraction wisdom teaches us is conducive to our own highest good. It doesn't matter if we're feeling in love with our own desires or feeling love for someone else. Love is love and it's always magnetic to our highest good. And it's easy to want the best for someone else without going into attachment and worry.

This kind of exercise fits the new-paradigm operating model perfectly: the investment in infrastructure is minimal, it is empowered by small contributions from masses of people and those small contributions become a large pool accessible to all. It's win/win and it makes achieving an outcome easier than having to do it alone. It's also nonlinear, operating more in accordance with a quantum world view of connected consciousness unlimited by Newtonian space-time in that it doesn't require all the individuals making up the resource pool to be present together in the same place or time. I offer up the example of the miracle experiment not as *the* new model for working with consciousness, but as one illustration of how easily this new operating model can be applied to spiritual and personal growth practices.

This model isn't just more efficient. Working this way can't help but change us. Just as the generation that has grown up with the internet is more psychologically tuned toward thinking globally, sharing resources, and working in egalitarian power structures, those who haven't need to catch up in order to be in alignment with the times. And it's the elders among us who still make up large parts of the hierarchical power structures that are making such profoundly important decisions for our world. For example, as I'm writing these words in June of 2016, "Brexit" has just occurred, surprising the world. The vote to separate Great Britain from the European Union was unexpected to many but, perhaps not so unexpectedly, was brought into being by older people holding separatist values, the younger generation voting overwhelmingly against it.

The collection of exercises in this book is designed to help you create personal success and wellbeing, but even more importantly, they teach the skills of Unity consciousness. We need these skills to thrive, not just survive, because, as we'll explore in the next chapter, surviving is no longer an option and won't save us from the crises of our era. Allowing your heart and mind to have an experience here will help you become part of a world that is coming together in a new paradigm of wellbeing which, ultimately, is the best defense against the breakdown of our times. And, of course, in the manner of the new paradigm, as you thrive, you help the world around you do the same.

Chapter 6: "Thrival" as the Path to Survival

As a new operating model permeates all aspects of human culture, we are rethinking our deepest assumptions about evolution, survival and life on this planet. Collectively, we've been long entrenched in the survival myth drawn from Darwinism in which the strongest survive on the backs of all the rest. This survival of the fittest story portrays all living creatures as separate individuals struggling in competition with each other. But, in spite of the resurgence of Ayn Randian ideology since the eighties, this Darwinian view of life is proving to be a false one.

Bruce Lipton, bestselling author of *Biology of Belief,* broke new ground in the field of biology by making the case that genes and DNA can be manipulated by belief. In his next book, *Spontaneous Evolution,* he challenges the assumptions of Darwinism, saying, "What we have failed to realize is that the real evolutionary principle is 'thrival of the fittest.' Those organisms that best fit the environment by contributing and supporting global harmony get to thrive while the others—well..." He goes on to say, "Paradoxically, this new level of cooperative awareness means maximum expression for the individual and maximum benefit for the whole."[1] In other words, in order for our plagued species to survive, we need to abandon survival strategies and aim higher; we must learn how to thrive.

Competition is so built into our ways of living and thinking that many people hold fast to a position that it's necessary because it makes us better and stronger. But does it really? Is competition part of a thriving life or does winning simply give us momentary relief, knowing that we've survived on top—for now? In an interesting article in the Huffington Post entitled "Don't Compete—Create,"[2] Jonas Ellison suggests that those who are truly at the top of their game, even athletes in competitive sports, are no longer competing—even though others may be competing again them—rather, they are simply doing what they do best in a state of full creative flow. He says, "When we compete, we aim to take from others what's already been created instead of creating something ourselves." But, "When we create, we become free."

Anyone who has ever lost themselves in a creative flow that brings forth your best has experienced how different this is from measuring oneself against another. The latter is based on the hierarchical constructs of the old order that identify better and worse, powerful and less powerful, winners and losers, and so on.

As an evolving species, as we shift into Unity consciousness and "thrival" mode together, we discover that everyone's highest good is interconnected. There is no me instead of you, or you instead of me, there is only we. This new form of "We" consciousness has nothing to do with a loss of individuality, as in tribal (or in its baser form, mob) consciousness. A tribal form of group-mind is still rooted in separateness, and eventually results in one tribal group of minds joining together against another. The rise of nationalism, xenophobia and hate groups in the United States and Europe in the 21st century is an example of this kind of tribal consciousness and reflects a last-gasp resurgence of old-order thinking. In the new paradigm of Unity, each individual is able to be more fulfilled *as an individual* by tapping into the resource of all of us together, beyond our differences.

Exercise: Creating a Thriving Life

So, at this turning point in human evolution, quite simply, the future is about thriving, not surviving. Striving to survive leads to breakdown, while cooperatively aspiring to thrive is what enables breakthrough—and if we're not aligned with the attitude and actions of thriving, we're going to sink into the struggle to survive and the breakdown that goes with it.

When I have introduced this idea to groups, I'm surprised by how many people say that they seldom give thought to the concept of thriving. As one woman put it, "My favorite expression is, "I'm just trying to survive!'" It's hard to create what we haven't even let ourselves think about, so, before we give attention to creating a thriving life, take a moment here to reflect on what thriving might mean for you.

Reflection on Thriving:

Take a moment to reflect... What does it mean to thrive? What do you imagine to be the elements of a thriving life? How does thriving feel and look different from surviving? How does it look and feel different from meeting a goal? Is thriving different from "success"? If so, how? Have you given much attention to thriving? If you feel that you're already thriving, what would it mean to be more powerfully thriving?

Imagine yourself now stepping into a thriving life. Imagine walking around in that life, trying it on for size. See what you do that's different; notice what your day is like in this thrival experience.

How does this life feel? Do you feel more relaxed and at peace? How does it change levels of stress and pressure? How does it affect your relationships and interactions with people? How does it affect how you feel about yourself? How does it affect your state of health? Does anything feel missing as you imagine yourself thriving?

More Questions for Thought

As you imagined yourself thriving, did you notice any part of you that felt more comfortable with struggle? For example, do you identify with the righteousness of the underdog role, or the adrenalized effort of "dog eat dog" competition? Or the certainty that if there is "no pain" there can be "no gain"? Do you have any sense that what you don't struggle for is less valuable? Is there any part of "thriving" that you define as being so lofty that it's out of reach?

Create Your Definition of Thriving

1. In writing, create a definition of your thriving life.

2. Read over what you've written and see what important aspect of thriving you might have left out of your definition. It may be something you omitted because you don't believe it's possible. It might be something that you never think to ask of life because you were never taught that you could.

3. Imagine that what you have just written is what you are now asking of life. Is it truly enough? Keep looking until you see past your own blind spots to anything you might have left out and add it in.

Miracle Experiment: Thriving Together

Relax your body and quiet your thoughts with some deep, slow breaths...

Now, imagine yourself able to reach out, beyond time and space to be with every other person who has in the past, is in the present, and will in the future participate in a miracle experiment. Let your mind stretch to include all the unknown thousands of souls who have joined around this miracle experiment intention. (You don't have to believe this to be possible, just imagine what it would feel like if you did.)

Imagine that we're all joining minds, bringing only our highest and best to the meeting, forming a pool of consciousness. Greet these others as friends: many, many, new-old friends... As we hold the intention to join in loving consciousness, feel your own energy lifted...

Let your heart open in caring and send a wave of love to this group of unseen helper-friends. Unconditional love is what calls forth miracles so step out of yourself for a moment—away from your own cares—and just imagine all the countless souls, all around the world, who, just like you, have known suffering and challenges; who have felt alone and afraid; who have struggled rather than thrived; and, just for a moment, let your heart break open in compassion for all these others.

Take a moment to love them as purely and completely as God does... and know that people all over the world are doing the same for you... This is how we tap the unlimited possibilities of the Universe and call forth miracles—not alone, but together...

Now, imagine yourself reaching out to one person in this network of joined hearts and minds. Imagine there is someone who needs your help. We all shine in a way that is uniquely our own. We all have our own unique vibration and gift to the world. The gift of us isn't just in our actions; it's in our very being. It's who we are, just as the sun shines— not by effort, but by nature.

Imagine there is someone in this miracle experiment network who can be helped by your special vibration of love.

You don't need to know where in the world this person is, or even where they are in time. Just imagine this person's soul light is calling out to you and you answer it by shining love and by holding an intention for this person that their highest good now unfolds...

You don't need to believe any of this, but imagine what it would feel like if you did believe, beyond a shadow of a doubt, that your love is powerful enough to change this person's life for the better. Perhaps providing a hand through a dark passage; maybe sparking the inspiration that will lead to their greatness; maybe helping them to release pain and dis-ease from their body, or to manifest some cherished heart's desire, or to simply find peace of mind. Imagine that your love somehow tips a balance in this person's life, allowing them to step beyond old patterns of limitation and struggle to taste the new energy of thriving. As the tiniest effort of flicking a light switch turns darkness into light, imagine that your love right now is creating as dramatic a shift for another person.

If we knew how powerful our love is, we'd probably want nothing more than to spend our lives using it. It's just our lack of faith in ourselves that keeps us from reaching out to one another with this most powerful gift. But we don't need to have full faith or belief for this work to be effective. In this moment, simply pretend that you are a world-famous miracle-maker and that your love is now raising this person out of struggle and into thriving. Imagine caring about this person as you would a most beloved child, and you have just what this child needs to be happy and whole. And you give it with joy, because the giving fills you up as much as it does this beloved soul.

Now imagine this person's joy and gratitude as they receive this gift of grace. Let the whole spectrum of their feelings ripple through you, as though you were the receiver as well as the giver, and you are overflowing with the excitement, the happiness, the love, the overwhelming gratitude, maybe even the tears of relief, and anything else that's part of this person's joy. Let it fill you up

As you reach out to this soul, directing your light to work on their behalf, imagine that there is someone in this network of souls who is reaching out to you in the same way: turning the light on for you, releasing you from familiar struggles into unknown ease.

And now picture everyone in this whole miracle experiment network—many, many people in all places and different times—and imagine each one of them shining light to someone in the network in a way that leaves no one out. See all of us connected in love in a way that is both intimately personal and universal, forming a beautiful pattern of connections.

Our joining, one to one to one, creates a unified energy that lifts all of us up, and each of us now has a special angel, someone in the network who is shining light just to us, channeling the full power of the whole in a way that personalizes this energy and make it particularly accessible. Feel what a gift this is… breathe… and let it in. Know that you're not alone in the pursuit of your own well-being and highest good. You have a whole team working on your behalf and one special angel lifting the weight of separateness from your shoulders…

You don't need to believe that any of this is real, just relax into it and imagine… And now, gently, lightly, let it go.

Take a few deep breaths and come back.

Section II:

Changing Practices

Our duty, as men and women, is to proceed as if limits to our ability did not exist. We are collaborators in creation.

Pierre Teilhard de Chardin

Chapter 7: What Did We Just Do? The Elements of a New Spiritual Practice

This new way of working with consciousness, as with this last miracle experiment exercise, isn't just a new self-help technique. It reflects a radical rethinking of the basic model for life on our planet.

Remember, in the new operating model, individuals are empowered beyond anything we've previously known through small efforts contributed by masses of us into an organizing infrastructure. The process is win/win; it's easy; it's the virtually limitless power of all of us together sharing rather than taking. It's nonlinear and nonhierarchical, behaving more in accordance with quantum laws than older Newtonian ones.

To apply this model to a new spiritual practice, let's go back to the last miracle experiment exercise and break down what we did. Essentially, the process went like this:

1. **Identify personal desires and intentions without getting overly attached to them.** Have a light, pleasant daydream about your goals, and let them go.

2. **Shine love into the collective.** This is simply an intention to love every individual in the collective and it's how we create a

significant resource through small contributions from many people, the currency in this case being consciousness. The idea of the miracle experiment and the focus of the different miracle experiment exercises create the simple infrastructure that organizes the intention and attention of many.

These contributions of consciousness create a field of energy, which comprises the pool required for the new operating model. The agreement among a group of people to hold a common, loving intention that supports each member's highest good sets up a sort of boundary that holds and concentrates this energy— like a vessel holding water. This creates far more energy for manifestation than a single mind working in isolation.

The well-known, modern-day biochemist, Rupert Sheldrake, best known for his concept of "morphic resonance" which suggests the existence of collective memory among species as well as the existence of telepathic interconnections between organisms, might call this a "morphic field." He coined this term to describe the cumulative memory of species as well as human systems of thought. According to Sheldrake, these fields exist beyond time and space, are developed through repetition, and make it easier— like a worn pathway—for all subsequent individuals to follow in the same pattern.[1]

3. **Activate the energy of the collective through compassionate empathy.** Compassionate empathy is a passionate and actively emotional form of love that powerfully connects us to this collective resource. Empathy transforms the abstract idea of caring for others into something personal and heart-felt. The way I suggest moving into a compassionate state goes a step further than simply caring about another and hoping for the best. The exercises here suggest vividly imagining another's joy as their

highest good unfolds for them, feeling it as if you were them and the joy was your own.

4. **Tap the amplifying power of group consciousness.** Over my forty-year career in group facilitation, I've witnessed close-up the amplifying power of group work. Healing, insights, altered states and personal growth breakthroughs of all sorts seem to come far more easily in a group than in one-to-one sessions with a healer, teacher, or counselor (which is why I gave up my individual practice decades ago). Science is beginning to document this effect as well. The research team of Robert Jahn and Brenda Dunne, whose extensive experiments show conclusively that conscious intention alone can affect matter, also found that bonded pairs of people could affect the random mechanism of a machine six times more powerfully than single operators could, suggesting the synergy possible in harmoniously joined minds.

Science writer and best-selling author Lynne McTaggart is also well-acquainted with this effect. She has become best known for her meticulous reporting on the amazing new science of consciousness and its seemingly limitless power, including a variety of studies demonstrating that when minds join together in loving intention, those individuals quickly come into resonance, where their brains, hearts and guts synch up with one another.

This effect seems present even when individuals are not together in the same space, as she discovered in her own research project. In her book *The Intention Experiment*, she called for volunteers to take part in her own consciousness experiment, asking them to focus on a highly specific result, such as growing a spider plant in a lab. In her next book, *The Bond*, she reports that even though participants were separated by time and space, each participating from their own computers all over the world and not even instructed to focus on each other, many reported, "*an overwhelming and palpable sense of oneness*" with other participants.[2] The group effect of minds joined in kindness seems to have a profoundly positive effect on all participants, not just the specific focus of their kind thoughts.

The miracle experiment format taps and directs this mysterious byproduct of group consciousness, aiming it toward the higher good of all members of the group and to the world beyond. As McTaggart says in the summation of her book, *The Intention Experiment,* "We are only beginning to understand the vast and untapped human potential at our disposal: the human being's extraordinary capacity to influence the world."[3] Who knows what we may discover in our experiments together here as we intend for no less than the miraculous?

5. **De-emphasize the pursuit of purely personal gain.** In this way of working, even though we have started with our own desire, which may well be what brought us to the collective experience in the first place, the primary focus in the exercise is on loving others and helping their highest good to actualize, while the effect is that we see our own highest good actualize. There's less need to pursue our own personal gain because everyone in the collective is holding intention around our gain for us. And the joined consciousness of many is far more powerful than one person's intention acting alone.

It's like the much-told spiritual story of heaven and hell, where the people in hell are seated at an abundant banquet table but are all struggling and starving because their spoons are too long to bring the food to their mouths. The people in heaven are at the same table, and have the same spoons, but everyone is feasting and celebrating because they're feeding each other. In the "heaven" scenario, no one needs to be concerned with their own survival, so they are free to fully experience the joy of giving. This is how we replace our habitual survival strategies with thriving ones.

6. **Hold an intention outside of linear time.** This expands the potential for joining with others in that it allows us to join in consciousness with people from the past and future. Working outside of time also allows results to come to us before we've done any practice by way of an intention we will hold in the future, as well as through the loving intentions of people in other points of linear time impacting us in our "now." As outlandish as this may seem, research on consciousness suggests that even linear time is no barrier to the effects of intention once our imagination has expanded sufficiently to embrace the possibilities. This is a big concept that we will explore more fully in another chapter.

This way of working with focused intention has some fundamental differences from older practices that can enhance their effectiveness but, perhaps more importantly, they change our way of thinking, bringing us closer to the unified, global consciousness that Pierre Teilhard de Chardin foresaw when he described the "superhuman." Some key features that characterize this new method as well as humanity's new paradigm include:

1. It is fueled by the power of joined, loving consciousness, not simply our own singular consciousness and effort.

2. It heals the duality of giving and receiving that is at the root of all scarcity. When giving to others becomes the path to serving ourselves, then taking for ourselves at the expense of others, or taking without including the good of others in the process,

becomes obsolete.

3. It operates in a nonlinear paradigm outside of time and space. The intention shared by the whole collective to send consciousness backward and forward in time opens vast possibilities for how and when outcomes can manifest.

4. It doesn't require that we "believe" in order to change results. According to the new science of consciousness, imagination and intention are enough to move energy. Belief isn't necessary. Furthermore, the amplified energy of the collective can help lift individuals beyond their personal limiting beliefs into a higher vibrational state where manifestation can occur.

5. It works through lateral power structures instead of hierarchical ones and is consequently less reliant upon teachers, teachings, and techniques. For example, the exercises in this book are powerful because of the contributions of all of you, the readers. My information and specific exercises simply provide the organizing infrastructure that allows a collective to come together and become productive—in much the same way that Wikipedia has created an infrastructure that would be nothing without the contributions of masses of individuals.

6. It utilizes and facilitates a new kind of love that is both personal and collective. The passionate experience of love felt for large communities of people we will never personally know is a new experience that helps move us beyond the familial and tribal, into a global experience of love.

A question that I've been asked only once but which feels significant enough to address is this: if we can affect one another through the miracle experiment intention, can we harm each other? My simplest answer is that if you think it will then don't work with these exercises.

Your expectancy of harm might just be strong enough to undermine the benefits. A strong intention that I have put around this work and have clearly articulated in the exercises is that "each of us [is] bringing only higher love to the whole" and that we are, "bringing only our highest and best." Think of this as a filter that raises us out of the flaws of personality and into the perfection of spirit. As articulated in the first chapter of *Holding a Butterfly*:

> *As we join minds, we leave behind the clutter of small, weak thoughts that so often cloud our attention and we rise into a Higher Mind that is wise and wonderful. In this Higher Mind, we amplify each other's power for good and automatically repel harm.*[4]

Larry Dossey, M.D. addresses in depth the possibility of doing harm through negative prayer in his book, *Be Careful What You Pray For...*, and comes to the wise conclusion that, "*The most reliable forms of protection against the negative intentions of others involve psychological growth and maturity; honoring the presence of the Absolute in our life; and cultivating our capacity for love.*"[5] I couldn't agree more.

Now let's continue on with our celebration of Unity.

Exercise: Your New Network

Quiet your mind for a moment and let your attention float free. Take a deep breath or two to help you transition to a soft, open mental state...

Imagine that something has profoundly shifted for you as a result of an amazing new resource being put at your disposal. It is much like when some new technology makes a big difference in your day-to-day experience—perhaps the difference your first smart phone made, where all of a sudden you had unlimited access to information, people and resources right in the palm of your hand. You were suddenly connected to a web of human thought and activity. Imagine this miracle experiment network of participants to be a higher octave of this.

Imagine that now you are connected to a web of loving consciousness that is at once personal and global. This energetic field of love positively affects your state of physical health, enhances your feeling of emotional well-being, and provides energy to manifest your dreams. There is an opportunity for ease that didn't exist before. As with your phone, all you need to do is keep it charged and turned on—in this case, you charge it with the energy of your love and turn it on with your attention. Through conscious intention, you are quite literally joined to a huge team of people who want you to succeed, and who pray for your highest good. There are now many people loving you, people whose existence you had not even thought to imagine before opening these pages.

Spend today living with this awareness. Find a physical touchstone to act as a reminder. It could be a palm-sized rock or piece of crystal, or better yet, use your smart phone. Let it remind you of the network of people who are now providing the resources for your transformation. You don't need to understand how this works any more than you need to understand all the workings of your phone. Just imagine that it is there for you, and it works for you. Let this touchstone remind you to stop from time-to-time in your day and take a moment to just feel the loving connection of energy flowing from you and to you from this vast network of people. Imagine yourself around the metaphorical feasting table of heaven, feeding and being fed, and be grateful.

Chapter 8: Compassionate Empathy

The many recent trends toward cooperation, collaboration and community are the more physical manifestations of a love vibration. Love is the drive to come together; to unify. What we are seeing in so many cultural trends may just be the manifestation of the seed planted at the Harmonic Convergence now coming of age.

In *Holding a Butterfly,* I presented some of the science related to love suggesting that the profoundly transformative light so frequently described by people who have had near-death experiences may just be the universal energy that quantum physicists call the Zero Point Field. The Zero Point Field, invisible to our physical senses, is an unlimited energy field that essentially comprises the underpinnings of all existence. It's a resource that, according to modern physicists, could potentially meet our energy needs beyond imagining if we can learn how to tap it.

This field contains wisdom as well as energy, with research into consciousness pointing to memory and information being stored in the Zero Point Field rather than the brain. If the light described by near-death survivors is, in fact, the rare human experience of the Zero Point Field, then this field is far from a neutral energy. Those who have clinically died and been revived, consistently describe it as the light of unconditional love. Putting glimpses from science together with accounts from these survivors suggests the existence of a limitless, invisible energy that is everywhere, contains all knowledge, and is the quintessential essence of love. This could be at the heart of what religions strive to define as "God." The limitless energy of the Zero Point Field that scientists are working to tap might have its easiest access simply through the human experience of love.

The measurable effects of love are well-documented, especially as it relates to physical healing. Dean Ornish, M.D. pointed out in *Love and Survival*, his book of medical research documenting an undeniable link between physical health and the experience of being loved, that any drug found to have an impact as statistically significant as love would be major news in every medical journal and news magazine. The state of consciousness we call 'love" may be something far more complex and potent than the spiritual, altruistic, romantic or sentimental associations we tend to have with it. It may be our most powerful resource for shaping our life and our world.

While the whole genre of law of attraction, New Thought, and personal growth teachings, not to mention virtually all religious teachings, have long taught the importance of love, we are just now evolving into a truer understanding of its power, and into the skills required to more significantly harness it.

Many metaphysical, spiritual, and healing practices suggest *sending* love to another. This involves giving attention to one's own heart, imagining light, warmth or imagery around this area radiating outward to another. This is a beautiful and powerful practice that can be done with anyone, anytime, with or without their knowledge and permission.

A new-paradigm version of this practice that gives it even more power is through the channel of compassionate empathy. As it's presented in the exercises here, instead of sending love to another person, which assumes distance between oneself and the other and affirms a paradigm of separateness rather than unity, the focus is on feeling within yourself all the joy you imagine another might feel when their highest good is realized. Instead of wishing the best for another, the focus is on imagining their feelings of happiness as though you were experiencing them yourself as them. It's a joining, or unifying, experience rather than a "sending" experience and one you will find woven into the many exercises in this book.

Imagining the fulfillment, gratitude and happiness you imagine others will feel as their desires manifest is a kind of prayer offered on their behalf and it has a beneficial effect. Growing evidence supports the power of nearly any kind of caring and compassionate thought aimed at another to have a positive effect. One study showed that even research assistants with no particular skill in focusing intention or instruction to focus intention, who simply hoped for the best outcome for their lab rats, had a positive effect on their subjects[1]. But the experience of oneness—of joining with another—seems to be the most potent state of all.

In studies of those known for their documented abilities to heal through energetic means—including miraculous healings of seemingly incurable conditions—what healers have most often reported about the healing state is not just the intention to "send" healing to another, but a sense of becoming one with the other[2].

As Lawrence LeShan reported in his classic book on healers and the healing process, *The Medium, the Mystic, and the Physicist,* a consensus of many of the healers he interviewed was that, "there must be intense caring and a viewing of the healee within a framework in which healer and healee could become one entity in a larger context without either one of the two losing their individuality."[3] This feeling of oneness seems to be an intrinsic part of what differentiates the realm of measurable results from the realm of miraculous results.

In our experiments here, passionately feeling another's joyful fulfillment as if it's your own is a way into this highly effective state of oneness and it positively impacts giver as well as receiver; it's not simply an act of service.

All law of attraction teachings place great emphasis on passionate feeling as the key to attracting what you desire. Cultivating this passionate, personal experience of fulfillment, even on behalf of another, is a powerful state of consciousness that draws like to like, attracting your highest good to you at the same time as it assists the other.

So many spiritually-aware people feel the burden of too much empathy, so much so that they take on the pain of those around them. Research suggests that cultivating compassionate empathy may well be a way to resolve the vulnerability of being overly sensitive and empathic.

One study, for example, conducted by Daniel Bateson, a doctor of both psychology and theology, showed that people who were exposed to clips of others undergoing painful medical procedures and asked to imagine how they would feel in the subject's place, felt distress, but those who were directed to put themselves in the patient's place to imagine what he or she was going through shifted into a place of compassionate empathy and concern. This compassionate state was no longer a painful experience for the observer. Instead of feeling passively acted upon by the negative stimuli of these scenes, those experiencing empathy transformed them into something positive[4].

This research suggests a difference between being unintentionally empathic by simply hurting with another person and of intentionally imagining what the other is feeling. The first state is rooted in separateness and survivalism—we experience another's pain from a "me" point of view so it hurts and feels threatening. The latter perspective *understands* another's pain and feels compassion, which lifts us out of separateness into a state of love.

A study of monks who practiced compassionate meditation where the focus is on the desire and readiness to help others release suffering, showed a high degree of gamma brain wave activity, which is a sign of a mind at peak performance, heightened happiness and even enhanced immune function.[5] Compassion is clearly a heightened stated of functioning that is highly beneficial to the one experiencing it. It's through this state of compassion that healers and others who assist those in dire circumstances are able to be helpful without being harmed. Through compassion, healers and care-givers can remain empowered to help while enjoying a beneficial state of personal high functioning.

But what about observing someone's good fortune? This generally wouldn't trigger the high levels of distress that watching someone in pain would. Many may well feel genuinely happy to see another succeed. However, if we are feeling personally unfulfilled, observing rather than joining another's happiness can trigger such low vibrational states as jealousy, feelings of scarcity, inadequacy, separateness and depression. By putting oneself in the place of someone experiencing joy and joining their happiness, the observer is better able to release a distressing state of mind and even benefit from the other's high vibrational state of joy. Try this for yourself:

Exercise: Joining in Good Fortune

See if you can recall a time when someone's joy had the effect of escalating your own feelings of emptiness. Maybe it was an experience of being single and lonely while your best friend couldn't stop gushing about a new romance. Perhaps it was triggered by seeing a colleague excel while you trod water. Any time you've watched someone luxuriating in something you've deeply wanted could be a trigger for this experience of emptiness.

As a situation comes to mind, shift your perspective from observing the other's joy to imagining being this person. Imagine that you have all the wonderful things that he or she has and are overflowing with the joy of it. Imagine this until your whole body is vibrating with good feeling and it brings a smile to your face.

✧✧✧✧✧✧✧✧

If you were able to feel the emotion of joyful fulfillment, you shifted a potentially low vibrational state into one more conducive to changing your own circumstances for the better. If you're feeling envious of others or not seeing a lot of good fortune in your own life, this can be a particularly helpful way to not only relieve the distress of jealousy but to intentionally borrow the consciousness of those whom you most envy to magnetize similar blessings to yourself.

All of these examples of compassionate empathy are win/win: the care-giver is able to help another while maintaining a peaceful state; the metaphysical practitioner is able to attract personal miracles while intending the best for others; the observer is able to celebrate the wins of others while borrowing a bit of that person's winning state of consciousness.

For the highly sensitive person, cultivating the ability to join with another this way can help shift from being the sponge, susceptible to emotional contagion, to being the oscillator, setting the rhythm of well-being for self and others. And, during times of concern over a loved one's wellbeing, compassionate empathy can also help transform worry about another into a healing experience that benefits both of you.

Exercise: Transforming Concern into Helpful Prayer

Bring to mind a person for whom you have concern and who you would like to help. It may be someone going through difficult circumstances or in need of healing. It could simply be someone whose wellbeing you care about. First, hold this person and their circumstances in your mind and wish the best for them. Do this with as much heart-felt sincerity as you can. Spend a moment with this and then notice how you feel.

Are you feeling at peace? Less concerned? Joyful? About the same as before you held this wish in mind? Just notice.

Next, hold this person in mind again and this time, imagine something wonderful happening for them. Don't try to impose your own agendas by filling in the details of what and how, simply imagine this person overflowing with positive feelings such as gratitude, joy, excitement, relief and peace because something wonderful has happened.

Now imagine how it would feel to be this person as they are experiencing some marvelous gift of grace. Let yourself join with this person empathically so you feel yourself overflowing with all the delightful feelings you imagine for them...

If you have allowed yourself to truly join empathically with this person's positive emotion at receiving some great blessing, you too will feel the happiness. You will have not only raised your consciousness to a state where you can be of greater assistance to another person, but you will have also accessed a state of mind that will naturally attract good things into your life.

✧✧✧✧✧✧✧

In giving attention to this person's experience of joyful transformation instead of to their pain and limitations, this process affirms and amplifies the potential for a joyful reality instead of focusing on whatever pain might seem most real in the moment. In another chapter we will explore this more deeply as a path of supporting another's healing. One caveat here, as in all work with intention, it's important not to go into it with a great deal of attachment to a specific outcome. If you are highly attached to another person's wellbeing and are trying to make them happy, healthy or successful through the force of your intention, you may be attempting to override their will, which isn't productive for either of you. In relationships where it's difficult to take your own needs, fears and agendas out of your prayer for another, then simply hold an intention for peace.

Exercise: Sharing Peace

First, breathe into your own state of peace. Take whatever time you need to put yourself into a peaceful place where you feel able to hand all worries up to a higher power. When you truly feel peace, let that state expand to include the other person—like an energy field that has grown big enough to include both of you. Next, imagine the other person's feeling of peace as if it is your own and hold an intention that the highest good comes to pass for both of you. End by entrusting them to their own path and destiny, safe in knowing that the highest good is now unfolding, without your needing to know what or when or how... Breathe... and let go.

❖❖❖❖❖❖❖❖

Compassionate empathy is very much in alignment with the new energy of our times because it is such a unifying experience. It heals the duality of observer and observed, and of giver and receiver. It resolves the Newtonian perception of us all as separate entities through an immediate experience of emotional oneness. Compassion lifts us into the new energy of win/win, benefitting both parties and diminishing the space between the two. As the Dalai Lama put it in a 2010 tweet, "If you want others to be happy, practice compassion. If you want to be happy, practice compass

Chapter 9: Healing the Duality of Giving and Receiving

The miracle experiment exercises demonstrate a process by which we receive through giving. The cultural trends toward cooperation, collaboration and offering service to the collective are catching on so quickly because these forms of giving promote greater receiving for all. As the duality of giving and receiving becomes irrelevant, so do value judgments that call giving good and taking bad. They are simply inevitable parts of an indivisible ecosystem. The impulse to work together for the highest good of all, be it in the form of heart-felt compassion or online collaboration, is essentially what takes us all higher.

However, we still live in a culture that has long been steeped in the harsh Darwinian reality myth that urges us to look out for ourselves because no one else will. Looking around at our world can provide plenty of evidence of a dangerous, dog-eat-dog reality where scarcity is fact and we must scramble for our share. This "reality" coexists alongside socially instilled morality teachings that tell us it's better to give than receive because giving is an altruistic sacrifice that makes us better people. Caught in this duality, is it any wonder so many of us experience life as a struggle?

Research is showing a deeper truth about giving. It's not just something to do for moralistic reasons, as Lynne McTaggart explains in *The Bond*,

"Caring about others, even strangers, is automatic and basic to our biology. In fact, a desire to help is so necessary to us that we experience it as one of our chief pleasurable activities."[1] Physically, our heart rate measurably slows, our autonomic nervous system relaxes, and we produce oxytocin, the hormone associated with loving, happy feelings. This translates into enhanced physical health and the state of mind that law of attraction teachings assert will make us magnetic to our personal desires.

Conditioned to believe that giving is good *and* that Darwinian survival of the fittest mythology is true, many of us have struggled to heal this duality of giving and receiving in our lives. Some of us have spent decades at it. Because we want to be good, moral people, we give, even as we experience the distress of scarcity. When I ask my audiences how many people are better at giving than receiving, invariably more than half raise their hands. Many of us have learned to be more comfortable with giving than receiving. In the Darwinian reality paradigm, one person's fortune must be at another's expense. Consequently, there can be a burden of guilt and obligation attached to receiving more than one's share.

In this paradigm, unconditional giving may feel good at first because giving is inherently pleasurable. But then, because we have limited our capacity to receive and because we feel the pressure to scramble for our own needs, we wind up feeling depleted. Ultimately, the result is breakdown, be it on a small scale of feeling low-level resentment or depression, or of catching every cold and flu that passes our way, or of some greater magnitude such as a major health challenge that creates the necessity to receive help. Perhaps we go to therapy, learn about codependency and self-love, and do our healing work where we strive to balance giving and receiving.

My audiences tend to be sophisticated and self-aware—and I consider you, the reader, to be among this group. They understand the importance of honoring themselves with self-love and yet at the same time have a profound awareness of the power of unconditional love, unconditional giving, and the spiritual reality of our Oneness. In recent decades there have been many books, practices, and support groups all teaching the importance of self-love, and just as many on the spiritual teachings of Oneness. I know of a New Thought spiritual center that hosts a twelve-step codependency group one night of the week and a "Oneness Blessing" class on the next. Many of the same people show up.

The well-known, modern-day spiritual text *A Course in Miracles*, is just one of many spiritual paths that guide us to see the spiritual reality present beyond the illusions of the physical realm. *A Course in Miracles* defines giving and receiving as being the same. This is a lovely idea until it comes time to practice it in the everyday of life. When we feel our own needs are not being met, it can be challenging to prioritize the needs of others. We may be able to rise to it in our highest state. A whole world of spiritual mind-training practices has evolved over centuries to help us bridge the duality between what we perceive and what we hold to be higher truth.

Yet, isn't it still hard? Hard to keep our attention on the positive and see beyond the illusions of our senses and sensibilities when our survival fears are triggered? Being a good person means being perpetually challenged to choose between the reality of fear, which can seem very real, and the reality of love, which can seem very abstract.

Sometimes people are able to reach out in love even in the midst of the most catastrophic circumstances, and that's when we become heroes and saints. Larry Dossey, M.D. makes a compelling case in his book, *One Mind*, that it actually might be easier to be heroic at the most catastrophic moments when personal risk is highest as it kicks us out of our everyday state of self-preservation and into an experience of the "One-Mind" where we go into such a heightened awareness of our oneness with one another that the other person's risk becomes the same as our own. He experienced this himself as a surgeon in Vietnam when he put his life on the line to save others without giving it a second's thought. He wrote, "Before going to Vietnam I swore I would never take risks, out of respect for my family and those who cared about me. But whenever instances like the crashed helicopter arose, these resolutions evaporated... There was no careful deliberation during these decisive moments, no weighing of consequences: just action."[2]

But does it have to take such extreme circumstances for us to easily, automatically, serve the collective? The problem is that it's not enough to balance giving and receiving, as in "I'll keep a healthy balance between caring for myself and caring for others," because this still forces our energy to be divided between self and others. We're giving or we're receiving. And, as mentioned, those of us who aspire to be good people are likely to give a little more than we receive.

Just think about it. How easy is it for you to let someone give you something without feeling a need to reciprocate? How easy is it to ask for something without first having to desperately need it?
Many of us have to reach a point of illness or crisis in order to feel deserving of assistance. This paradigm of divided energy that emphasizes "me" or "you" but rarely evolves into "we" is what keeps scarcity in place, and conventional law of attraction teachings unwittingly perpetuate it.

The whole process of imagining our desires, getting excited about them, striving to believe they will manifest, then struggling not to have negative thoughts when they don't show up right away is a rather self-absorbed experience that keeps us firmly locked in "me" consciousness. When we live in the paradigm of duality that separates giving and receiving, one that separates "me" and "we," it's always going to be a challenge to act on behalf of the whole.

When we start to experience loving and serving the collective as also being the most efficient means of fulfilling our personal needs and wants, it ceases to be hard. We don't have to be a hero or a saint risking life and limb. We simply set a different reality paradigm in motion.

But before we can truly move into this new reality paradigm where giving and receiving are indivisible, many of us need to do some healing around receiving and unlearn some of the limited perceptions that no longer serve. There's no use in creating an abundance of anything good for ourselves if we have difficulty receiving it. I've experienced this myself when I first encountered metaphysical principles of attraction. Before I did some personal work around receiving, I had a number of experiences where the techniques worked wonderfully, bringing sudden windfalls of money into my life, but instead of leaving me happy and grateful, I felt rather guilty and burdened by it all.

Receiving is a key, yet often overlooked, aspect of empowerment. It's easy to become so fixed on a goal and the process of achieving it that we forget to be receptive.

We may even unconsciously deflect what we most want without realizing it. If you often feel burned out, that you're doing too much alone, that your efforts are greater than the rewards, and that you're somehow missing out on the joy of life, you may be forgetting to receive.

Receiving isn't simply about accepting what we want when we want it, on our own terms. I've often seen people think they have no problem with receiving—it's just that what they want hasn't shown up yet! These folks are often holding out for the big prizes they've set their sights on while deflecting dozens of small gifts each day. The energetic universe around us is highly responsive to our desires and state of being and, ultimately, won't give us more than we can bear to receive. Consequently, until we can bear to accept the small gifts that come our way, we won't be burdened with bigger ones.

If life's big gifts are eluding you, ask yourself: when someone compliments you, do you appreciate it and say thank you, or do you deflect it in some way? Do you look away, make a joke, or say something self-deprecating? If someone offers to buy you lunch, do you graciously receive it, automatically refuse, or accept but feel uncomfortably indebted? When you receive presents, do you enjoy them, or are you hard to please with gifts? Is your mind so busy with thoughts of what you'll have to give back in reciprocation that it diminishes your pleasure in the receiving? When someone offers to help you, do you gratefully receive it or insist that you can manage alone? (Do you assume you can manage alone more easily than with help?) And, when someone loves you, do you feel blessed by this most precious gift, or do you retreat in fear? Do you find the love of only a specific few to be valuable and fail to appreciate the many others who may care about you?

If you're starting to recognize in yourself any of these signs of poor receiving, you're not alone. Whenever I poll groups of people on the subject, I'm struck by how common a problem it is.

In one of my larger group sessions, I once held a brainstorming session, asking people to identify all the reasons they could think of as to why they experienced discomfort around receiving, both in the personal sense of receiving from others as well as in the broader sense of receiving their highest good from life. After receiving dozens of responses, I noticed themes that came up again and again. Here they are, organized into categories with their variations listed. See if any of these feel familiar to you.

Reasons We Resist Receiving

1. Guilt: I don't deserve it.

- I'm not good enough.
- There's only so much of anything good to go around. It's not fair for

me to get more than my share.

- No one deserves a free ride. I need to work hard for what I get.

2. There are too many strings attached.

- Receiving creates unwanted obligations to reciprocate. The more I receive, the more people expect from me.
- People give because they want something from me and I feel manipulated when I receive these gifts.

3. Having an abundance of good things makes me feel separate.

- Will people still love me if I'm happy/successful/prosperous/powerful/have more than they do?
- Will I still get attention/support/love if I don't need it?
- Rich people/powerful people/successful people are awful. I don't want to be like them.

4. Receiving creates vulnerability in relation to others.

- Receiving from others makes me feel needy and weak.
- If I become reliant on someone giving to me, they have more power to hurt me. (I'm the only person I can trust.)
- If I do all the giving, I stay in a one-up position of control. They owe me. I can feel connected without feeling vulnerable.

5. No faith in others.

- No one can take care of me as well as I can.
- Letting other people help just makes more work for me.
- I can't trust people to do as good a job as I do.

6. Fear of the unknown.

- What if I get what I want and I'm still not happy?
- What if I get everything I want, am blissfully happy and then lose

it? That would be more devastating than never having it to begin with.

- What if I get the opportunity I've always wanted and blow it? Dreaming of what could be might be better than getting a chance and failing.
- It's too upsetting to my assumption about reality: receiving something better than I believe is possible can be too mind-boggling to accept. It feels safer to hold onto the security of reality as I know it.

7. Loss of special identity: having less defines me and receiving something better from life would mean losing some integral aspect of how I see myself.

- I'm a struggling survivor/impoverished artist/activist/ victim/addict/underdog, etc. (fill in the blank). It's part of what makes me special (or what makes me part of a special group). Who would I be and who would be my community without this defining me?

8. A sheer lack of vision.

- We've been conditioned by life experience to disbelieve that what we want exists.
- We've been conditioned to avoid wanting too much or even imagining having what we want. Why dream about what I can't have?

Questions for Thought: Giving and Receiving

- How are you at giving and receiving? Do you experience yourself as giving more than you receive, receiving more than you give, or do they seem in balance? Or, do you feel outside the flow of giving and receiving, not doing much of either?

- What is more comfortable/less comfortable to receive: money, gifts, attention, acknowledgment, love, affection, help?

- In the areas where you've identified some discomfort around receiving, what are the reasons underlying your resistance?

✦✦✦✦✦✦✦✦✦

Even though we're looking at receiving here as though it can be separated out from giving, the bigger truth is that they can't really be separated from each other any more than inhaling and exhaling can be. Just as inhaling and exhaling flow together as breath, giving and receiving flow together as joining.

This means that if we're not very good at receiving, we're not good at giving either—even if we've always thought of ourselves as generous and as giving more than our share.

When we give without receiving we're denying the opportunity for joining in love. Think of how disappointing it is to give to someone who doesn't fully appreciate and receive the gift. When we don't receive, we may be sharing our generosity, but we're withholding the greater gift of connection. If our giving doesn't create joining in love, then it's not a true gift. We may be giving to feel good about ourselves, to get something back, or to control the other person.

The next miracle experiment is to expand your capacity to receive, and to offer up your willingness to receive as the highest of gifts. So, relax, breathe, and get ready to receive...

Miracle Experiment: Opening to Receive

*Relax your body and quiet your thoughts with some deep, slow breaths...
Let your sense of identification shift from the density and limitation of
matter to a bright, clear, beautiful energy that is your true essence. As
you make this shift in perception you leave behind the limitations of
dense matter and start to see the cells of your physical body lighting up
and becoming radiant with this energy... And now, all the particles that
make up your body are becoming lighter; the molecules, the atoms, the
sub-atomic particles, all spreading out, vibrating in beautiful light.*

*See the bright energy of everyone in this miracle experiment network of
souls vibrating together now, in joined consciousness beyond the
illusionary limits of space and time, each of us bringing only higher love
to the whole.*

*You might imagine us all meeting in a magnificent, sacred arena in the
spiritual realm, or see us forming a wave-like circle of energy, or web of
light. See this joining as beautiful, sacred, awe-inspiring, and filled with
the potent energy of love. As a group, we form a powerful network for
healing and miracles.*

*Recognize how much more powerful we are together than we could ever
be separately. Our joined intentions quicken our growth, awaken our
intuition and heighten our magnetism to our highest good. What has
seemed difficult in the past will come more easily now. Take a moment
to feel the light and energy of the network building...*

*Now, imagine the energy of the Universe. Name it as you like: the Zero
Point Field, the One Mind, Love and Light... Picture this as a field that is
all around you and within you; an ever present, invisible sea of light that
contains unlimited potential. What's more, it is inherently intelligent and
kind.*

Feel the very air around you to be alive and filled with love. Feel it holding you safe and secure, like a loving parent holding the most precious child. Relax completely and softly into this loving energy just like a small child filled with complete trust...

Now you've tapped God energy. This energy is having a very real effect on you, body and mind. If you're in need of healing, this will give you a boost. Don't try to focus on anything, just be like a tiny child, completely relaxed in loving arms. Relax... breathe... and receive...

Place your hand on your own heart and feel it there, warm and comforting. Take in the feeling of this touch more deeply than you ordinarily would. Reassure yourself, as this energy of God would, that you deserve to receive love, joy, and all forms of God's bounty and grace.

Now, as you hold your heart, imagine a comforting, loving hand on your back over the area of your heart. Imagine that a kind, loving soul from this network of miracle experiment participants has come to you in service, to channel Universal love to you. You might even feel more than one hand as multiple souls come to you as helper spirits right now.

You don't even need to believe that this is real, just imagine it and make it real in your mind's eye. We are far more connected to each other than we consciously know. The love that you're receiving is completely unconditional. There's nothing you need to do to earn it or deserve it. Feel the presence of this touch softening, comforting and awakening your heart center.

The love coming through offers silent reassurance that you are worthy, you are valued, you are deserving of God's love and abundance. Relax... breathe... and receive... Let yourself be washed in love.

Let love wash away anything you no longer need: dis-ease of body and mind, and most especially the protective armoring that's grown around your heart. Let love wash away these walls that keep you locked in separateness, inhibiting your ability to receive and take joy in life. Let it all be melted away in this flood of healing love. Completely surrender to the sensations in your body. Don't think, just feel, be present... breathe... receive... You don't need to believe or understand any of this, just be present in your body and allow yourself to be cared for, valued and loved.

Now hold in mind any resistance you've ever had to receiving from life—any feelings of being unworthy, that you shouldn't take more than your share, that you haven't earned this attention or that you should be able to take care of yourself without the support of others—and breathe... past... your... resistance... Stretch open to receive...

As you break through any resistance you have to receiving, you are helping all of us to break through the outmoded beliefs that keep us all in scarcity. You are helping everyone to break through old patterns of survival so that we may all thrive together. You have become the giver, so receive even more... Let the walls of fear and defense melt so that God's love can penetrate... Know that if you can do this, so can we all...

Feel how much energy it takes to keep on with the struggle to survive and maintain the walls of defense... Feel the freedom, the softness, the lightness of letting it all go. Let yourself overflow with relief and joy and perhaps even tears of gratitude as you finally relax and surrender to love and all the miracles that go with it... As you feel this breakthrough in yourself, know that we are feeling it with you...

So now reach out in compassionate empathy to someone in our vast network of souls who has never felt worthy until this moment and is finally realizing how much they are loved by God and deserving of all God's gifts.

Imagine how this person now feels to have long resisted receiving the goodness of life and is finally letting it all in. Imagine that you are reaching through time and space, placing your hand ever so gently on their back over their heart. Silently reassure this soul that they are deserving and valued and loved. Feel with this soul their great relief as they let down burdens of separateness they didn't even know they were shouldering.

Feel the joy as we all relax into the goodness of life...

Take a deep breath to bring yourself back... and don't be surprised if you start noticing more and more that life is good.

Chapter 10: We Don't Have to "Believe" in Order to Change Results

If you are familiar with law of attraction teachings, you may have often heard that it's necessary to change your beliefs in order to change your results. In my experience, this simply isn't true. If you are a dedicated student of New Thought spirituality, this very assertion may challenge your beliefs. But, without needing to believe, try this exercise:

Exercise: Your Impossible Dream

Bring to mind something that you would like to have or experience but believe is out of reach. Make it something important to you that you would like to manifest but see no clear path toward at this time.

Knowing that it's probably impossible, close your eyes and let yourself have a light, pleasant daydream of what it would be like if this did come to pass. You don't have to believe it can happen, just enjoy the daydream. In your daydream, let this reality remain in the realm of impossibility where you don't hold any agendas around trying to make it yours. Simply enjoy it. Don't strain or try to make this into serious work, just have fun with it... and when the daydream reaches a natural completion, let it go.

What if that's all you need to do to? Were you expecting more of an exercise? Maybe thirty days of affirmation work, a burning ritual, or at least a longer visualization? If you need more, then write a brief description of what you daydreamed about, fold up the paper and put it away in a place where you can forget about it for six months or so.

In my decades of experience with consciousness-based practices, I have found that it's not necessary to "believe" in order to manifest results. One simply needs to imagine in an open, light frame of mind. While beliefs are certainly important, just as proceeding step by step is still a viable route toward a goal, so does it still hold true that changing our beliefs impacts our reality. It just isn't the only route. And changing a belief system can feel like climbing Mount Everest, while a free and easy daydream can happen in the blink of an eye. Here's an example of this from my own life.

The first property I ever bought was too impossibly beautiful and expensive for me to own but it fell into my hands without my even needing to draw from my own personal funds. All I did was see this property and think about it. I didn't believe for a minute that buying it was a possibility.

I was shopping for a multi-apartment building with a friend. We had a vision of living cooperatively with one or two other friends but all the properties we were seeing were shabby, expensive, and felt nothing like home. After a depressing shopping excursion, my friend invited me to her home in a big, stately Victorian mansion where she rented a tiny apartment. The house was magnificent and well-kept by the owners who lived on the first floor. This building was everything we wanted, and it made all the other properties seem even shabbier by comparison. But it wasn't for sale and, if it had been, it would have been way beyond our budget. All the same, I couldn't get the beautiful woodwork, light-filled rooms, and fabulous garden out of my mind. It was so out of the range of possibility that I didn't get attached to it; but I also couldn't get it out of my mind.

The next week, the need to find a new home became urgent—I received notice that the apartment building where I was living was being sold and that I had to be out in thirty days. This happened just as I was about to lead a five-day intensive, which meant I would have no time to look for another place to live until the next week. Fortunately, being completely absorbed in a workshop left little opportunity to worry about it.

The day after my workshop ended my friend called to say she had news, and that I might want to sit down. She had been talking to her landlady who casually mentioned that she was getting tired of being a landlord and might think about selling someday. My friend responded that we might be interested in buying and the conversation quickly evolved into an agreement to sell to us as soon as possible. What's more, because we were open to her and her husband staying in their first-floor apartment as renters for as long as they needed while they built their dream home, she offered us a price that was about $150,000 under market value—and completely within our budget.

Everything flowed from there. The tenants living in the third-floor apartment I coveted had already given notice that they would be moving just as I needed to be out of my apartment, so I was able to rent from the sellers for a month while we got our financing in order. And as for financing, because the selling price was so far under market value, we were able to get a loan for the whole amount plus $6000 extra so that we would have some money in reserve for maintenance. Because we just happened to be the recipients of the first business loan offered by a new department of our credit union, we got a lot of special attention and mentoring as well as a special rate that they never offered again.

In effect, with a lot of signatures and no personal funds invested, this giant building was simply turned over to us. Neither of us knew a thing about taking care of a creaky, old property but since the owners didn't move out right away, we had almost a year of mentoring where we learned all the how-tos of property maintenance and management. There were so many fortunate "coincidences" that followed quickly on the heels of my daydreams—and I've seen this happen so often for myself and others—that I can't simply write it off as good luck, unrelated to consciousness.

Holding a Butterfly is filled with such anecdotes and a bit of the science explaining these miraculous coincidences. If you find yourself doubting the connection between intention and manifestation, I refer you there for a deeper dive. Even if you are an enthusiastic believer, reading these stories of others' successes and miracles will give you a heart-opening boost into miracle-consciousness. If you are a skeptic, the good news is, as I'm suggesting here, that you don't need to believe in order to see positive results. Imagination and open-mindedness are enough. I suggest adopting an experimental frame of mind. Conduct your own trials with these exercises, see what happens, and draw your own conclusions.

So, what exactly happens in a short little daydream that doesn't happen in hours of more focused manifesting exercises? For one thing, the nature of a daydream is pleasant. Unlike an exercise designed to create a result, a daydream has no agenda-driven quality of working toward a goal. In fact, it's more of an escape from "work."

Working toward a goal is a linear process; it proceeds step by step, and it may or may not be pleasurable. Working toward a goal this way is very effective in many contexts, but the process can break down when applied to the nonlinear realm of metaphysics because this realm doesn't operate according to linear rules. Using consciousness in a more intentional way is a delicate process of lifting out of linear reality and tapping into quantum reality. This is a highly pleasurable experience characterized by such states as joy, love, inner peace, compassion, unity, transcendence and ecstasy.

Step-by-step metaphysical exercises are meant to take us there, but when applied in a heavy-handed way through the filters of linear thinking, they can become work rather than pleasure. Exercises in consciousness that don't ultimately take us to a state that feels light and good are probably not doing what we intend them to do. Ironically, sometimes a simple little daydream can have more of the magnetic pleasure-consciousness than hours of dedicated "work."

Something that is less likely to happen in a daydream is attachment. In fact, if we believe that something is out of reach, it's even easier to remain unattached. When I spontaneously envisioned the beautiful building I had fallen in love with, I had no expectation that I would ever own it. I wasn't trying to make it mine. Once we put energy into convincing ourselves that we "believe," we can manifest something, we're a lot more invested in seeing our belief manifest. Then, of course, we are attached. Attachment is the antithesis of an effective manifesting state because it's not pleasurable.

Pleasurable daydreaming without attachment is a way to try on new realities, to walk around in them and see how they fit. They can be a powerful part of our creativity and a way that we move into new realms of experience—by projecting our consciousness there first.

Daydreams can, of course, cross the line into obsessive thinking, which happens when we fantasize with a high level of attachment. Then fantasy becomes an addiction. A good way to discern the difference between unattached, creative daydreaming and addictive fantasy is how it leaves us feeling. Addictions always create more craving for the addictive experience because it's an attempt to fill a void with something that won't ever leave us feeling fulfilled. Consequently, an obsessive fantasy leaves us feeling empty and craving more and more fantasy. By contrast, a daydream is light, can be released easily without leaving a well of longing, and gives a moment of pleasure in the experiencing.

Seeing the physical world respond to the light and joyful vibration of our unattached daydreams can build faith in this process, even if we didn't start out as a "believer." And faith is a very potent state for shifting physical reality. As the master metaphysician Jesus taught, we only need a mustard seed's worth of faith to move a mountain (Matthew 17:20). When we have faith, we no longer need belief.

I've had many a debate with folks trying to convince me that faith and belief are the same, and it's true that these words are often used interchangeably. To clarify, I am referring here to "belief" as I once saw it defined in a dictionary: "Belief may suggest mental acceptance without directly implying certitude or certainty on the part of the believer." Other dictionary descriptions included "opinion" and "conviction." In other words, it's a mental construct we have formulated; an interpretation of reality that we have an attachment to; an opinion that becomes conviction. We often feel threatened when our beliefs are challenged. On the other hand, faith comes from certainty based on knowing and it's free of attachment. An excellent and succinct definition of faith found in the Bible is that, "...faith is the substance of things hoped for, the evidence of things not seen." (Hebrew 11:1.) Note that this says the "substance" and "evidence," not the hope and wish for things unseen.

Faith can also include things we simply know deep inside before we've seen physical evidence. In *Holding a Butterfly*, I recounted the story of a young man who decided to move to a big city, showing up homeless, jobless, penniless, and friendless. He kept saying to himself, "I don't know what's going to happen, but I know it's going to be great!" He wasn't doing this as an affirmation technique to convince himself. It was a purely spontaneous and joyful response to his experience of the unknown. And with astonishing speed and serendipity, one thing after another fell into place for him: a place to stay, a job, friends, and soon his new life was well underway.

The big difference between saying this declaration as a belief and saying it from faith is that with faith, there is a powerful feeling of certainty in the moment with no need to defend it to others who don't share it. If someone had come along and told him he was crazy to do what he had done; that something awful might well happen, he probably would have just laughed and carried on. That's faith. If he merely "believed" in his declaration, the same challenge would be more likely to provoke a reaction of defensiveness, irritation, self-doubt and worry.

I'm not proposing that we bypass the work of personal and spiritual maturity for a quick fix promising a perfect life. Spiritual maturity is a journey of a life-time and brings joy, peace and wisdom. I am simply suggesting that sometimes the bigger challenge in calling forth a result is in how easy it is rather than in how much work it requires. I've known many dedicated students of New Thought teachings who try to white-knuckle their way into the "right" beliefs, applying discipline, control and endless practices, and in so doing, ultimately bring doubt and fear into a process that must be light and pleasurable if it's to be effective. Too much hard work can also lead to becoming insular and caught up in our own small desires—not an effective manifesting state. Trying hard to hold the right belief and not the wrong one can become a little like trying not to think of an elephant. Letting go of the prerequisite of belief takes a lot of pressure off.

Another story from *Holding a Butterfly* was that of a woman in my workshop who was instructed to think of the two most impossible things she would like to heal. She identified two things and she legitimately believed they were out of the question. Within twelve hours she had manifested both of them, including being free of pain and her cane for the first time in ten years since a crippling car accident.

Does this mean that libraries of metaphysical and New Thought teachings that emphasize the importance of belief are wrong? No. It simply means that just as the new operating model of our times is creating options, pathways and resources that were never available before, evolutionary shifts have created new wrinkles in teachings that once seemed carved in stone.

One such evolutionary change in recent decades is our expanded human capacity to comprehend nonlinear realities. This includes thinking outside of time, which we'll explore further in Chapter Twelve, as well as our ability to simply disconnect from the automatic mental filter that strives to find a linear path to every outcome, even spiritual ones (as in, if I meditate/visualize/write affirmations, etc. long enough, I will get what I want).

Another thing that has changed, and this is more the focus of our work here, is the added resource of all of us together. When you achieve states of pleasure, love, compassion, connection and peace, your beliefs *will* change, and you will manifest more of what brings you joy. You won't need to try so hard to make these things happen.

With that, let's sail away into the next miracle experiment. Faith is not only a potent manifesting state, it's also highly contagious, and one person's faith can spark another's. A group of people with faith can lift even nonbelievers to a state of miracle-consciousness like a river lifting all proverbial boats together, so relax, breathe, and let your mind float free. Don't try to believe; just imagine...

Miracle Experiment: Raising Faith

Go back to the light daydream you held at the beginning of this chapter. Bring it to mind in a way that it feels pleasant...

Now, imagine yourself able to reach out, beyond time and space to be with every other person who has in the past, is in the present, and will in the future read these words... Then let your mind stretch further to include all the unknown thousands of souls who have joined around this miracle experiment intention. (You don't have to believe this to be possible, just imagine what it would feel like if you did.)

Imagine that we're all joining minds, bringing only our highest and best to the meeting, forming a pool of consciousness. As we hold the intention to join in loving consciousness, feel your own energy become light and buoyant.

Imagine each of us having a sweet daydream of something that feels out of reach. Each of us is having a pleasurable moment in this daydream. Maybe you can see all kinds of relaxed, smiling faces caught up in a moment of happy dreaming...

In your imagination, search this whole group of souls until you sense one particular individual who has the remarkable experience of their impossible daydream manifesting in a form even more perfect than they envisioned.

Even if you don't have faith that this will happen for yourself, even if you don't have faith that this will happen for many of us, see if you can have absolute faith that it will happen for someone, and tune in to that individual. You don't need to see the details of who and what and how. Just tune in to the emotional experience this person is having as their impossible daydream comes to life. Put yourself in his or her place as this amazing reality unfolds, feeling the joy and exhilaration...

Feel with this person the empowerment of seeing the universe respond so powerfully to an easy mental state. And feel this person's growing sense of faith that it's possible to have this experience again...

As you are filled with all these wonderful feelings of joy, faith and empowerment that you imagine this other to be experiencing, you too are now holding the magnetic vibration of empowered faith, so, let your mind reach out to all the others in our network who don't have faith that miracles can happen for them.

Picture all of those with lagging faith as holding unlit candles. You can see that some in our network have more faith than others, and these folks appear holding lit candles. As you imagine this, what is the proportion of lit candles to unlit? More than half of us? Less than half? Let your imagination fill in the details of how much faith we collectively have. Don't try to force it, just observe...

Now, with the vibration of faith still strong in you, give a light to some of the unlit candles you see and imagine others with lit candles doing the same until everyone is alight together. This is easy, because a candle doesn't lose any of its own fire by lighting other candles. See all the lit candles sharing this way and let this be an easy and playful daydream, not hard work. As every candle lights, feel a spark of joy vibrating in you...

Finally, go back to your original daydream—your own "impossible" dream... Bring it lightly to mind. Laugh with pleasure over it... and let it go as easily as you would release a butterfly that lit in your hand. Now, briefly, just for fun, imagine several other impossible scenarios that you might enjoy having manifest in your life. Don't strain, just enjoy... and then let them go.

To complete this exercise, recognize that everyone who has ever or will ever do this exercise has just held faith for you. You have just given and received the powerfully magnetic vibration of faith. There is no need to worry about whether or not it will work, just be grateful.

Chapter 11: Collective Intelligence

Collective intelligence is the intelligence that results from a group working together. It's certainly not a new phenomenon—as a social species, we've always worked together in groups for survival, efficiency and comfort. What's new however, is the massive scale of collective intelligence that has so quickly emerged as a result of the unprecedented global connectivity of the internet.

In 2006, the "hive-mind" effect created by millions of people and millions of computers all connected to one another inspired the creation of a new research center at the Massachusetts Institute of Technology: the Center for Collective Intelligence. Headed by Thomas W. Malone, the mission of the center is to explore how this collective mind of people and computers just might be able to *"act more intelligently than any individual, group, or computer has ever done before."*[1]

Malone recognizes that the amazing, new access to information and to each other that we now have only scratches the surface of things to come and he is exploring how collective intelligence can be tapped to address such pressing problems as global climate change.

He explains in a 2012 interview in Edge.org, an online magazine of cutting edge science and ideas:

"...think of Wikipedia, where thousands of people all over the world have collectively created a very large and amazingly high quality intellectual product with almost no centralized control. And, by the way, without even being paid. I think these examples of things like Google and Wikipedia are not the end of the story. I think they're just barely the beginning of the story. We're likely to see lots more examples of Internet-enabled collective intelligence—and other kinds of collective intelligence as well— over the coming decades."[2]

In a short amount of time—the time since the Harmonic Convergence— we have created a global, technological membrane that holds all the knowledge of the world and connects the active thinking of billions. As Malone put it, *"As all the people and computers on our planet get more and more closely connected, it's becoming increasingly useful to think of all the people and computers on the planet as a kind of global brain."*

Paralleling this development in the early 1990s, just as the internet was picking up steam and creating this global brain, the work of a number of scientists was coalescing into the astonishing new understanding of the Zero Point Field as being the repository of all memory and information rather than the brain.

Lynne McTaggart wrote of this scientific development in *The Field,* *"Some scientists went as far as to suggest that all of our higher cognitive processes result from an interaction with the Zero Point Field... [which] might account for intuition or creativity..."[3]*

So, while scientists were bringing to light the profound nature of our interconnectedness through this One Mind of the Zero Point Field, we were creating a precise technological replica of the One Mind in the form of personal computers connected via the internet. The latter made a radically new experience of connection commonplace in an amazingly short amount of time. Might these parallel occurrences related to One

Mindedness be part of the same evolutionary pull to Unity planted just a handful of years earlier in 1987?

In his 2013 book, *One Mind*, Larry Dossey, M.D. offered a wide range of anecdotes and science illustrating the many ways that minds are remarkably connected beyond time, space and natural law as we think of it. He describes the One Mind as a state where we all meet, but also as a resource we may each tap into for "a transcendent moment, an epiphany, or creative breakthrough."[4] Dossey wrote the book because he believes we are in "no ordinary times" and that the experience of the One Mind is urgently needed in order to escape "the division, bitterness, selfishness, greed, and destruction that threaten to engulf our world."[5]

Dossey's description of the One Mind and McTaggart's description of the Zero Point Field are very similar, and not dissimilar to the kind of internet-generated collective intelligence described by Thomas Malone: "...a field of knowing that is greater than that of any group member and greater than the sum of a group's members," and that includes "heightened imagination and creativity." [6]

There's no denying that many untruths and ugliness are propagated via the internet, leaving many wondering if it's furthering or countering our evolution. Certainly there are ways in which it has amplified some of our darker human tendencies. There is a key factor however, that characterizes and differentiates this newly emerging form of collective intelligence from what we've known before, and that is anonymity combined with mass participation.

Wikipedia is an example of this model. While its contributors aren't truly anonymous, the model works because there are many unpaid contributors who contribute for the sake of contributing rather than for payment or recognition. Even an infrastructure as well-known and wide-spread as Wikipedia doesn't produce superstars among its tens of thousands of contributors.

Another particularly interesting example of this kind of anonymous participation is the loosely organized, international, anarchistic group of uberhackers and geeks known as "Anonymous." Anonymous started in the early 2000s with the focus of preserving free speech on the internet but has grown increasingly activist. In reaction to the corruption and dysfunction of traditional governing bodies, Anonymous has taken on policing violations of freedom around the world with a Robin Hood/Trickster kind of flare.

How does it operate without an organizational structure? Quinn Norton explains it well in an article he wrote for the online magazine *Wired*, in July of 2012, entitled "How Anonymous Picks Targets, Launches Attacks, and Takes Powerful Organizations Down." Norton writes:

> *In fact, the success of Anonymous without leaders is pretty easy to understand—if you forget everything you think you know about how organizations work. Anonymous is a classic "do-ocracy," to use a phrase that's popular in the open source movement. As the term implies, that means rule by sheer doing: Individuals propose actions, others join in (or not), and then the Anonymous flag is flown over the result. There's no one to grant permission, no promise of praise or credit, so every action must be its own reward.*[7]

In other words, the anonymity of the internet takes ego out of the process. In its short history, Anonymous has hacked into the highest level of governing from the Vatican (for its teachings on birth control and abortion as well as its handling of sexual abuse scandals) to the Chinese government (aiming at the Great Firewall of China, the government's very complicated system of internet censorship), to the U.K. government (to protest proposals to monitor all web and phone traffic).

Whether you find the anarchistic power of Anonymous terrifying or refreshing, it clearly is the antithesis of hierarchical power, having no leader and an internal structure that has often been likened to a flock of birds. As one person describes it on an Anonymous forum: "Each bird is free to go where he wishes, in any direction, can join any flock with any cause, or form his own flock, with his own cause. The most successful causes/operations have the largest number of anons following along."

The formless nature of Anonymous means, of course, that it is ever-changing. What's to stop it from morphing into a world-wide, hierarchical organization swayed by a charismatic evil-doer? Well, nothing except a new uprising of "birds" moving in a counter direction. Is it possible that the very nature of this kind of anonymous hive mind is to be self-regulating, forever moving in the direction of the many instead of the one?

When power-driven egos are taken out of the equation and leaders are unable to emerge, could there be something inherently true about the will of the collective that sends the majority of us flying in whatever direction serves the highest good of all?

Anonymous is raw and crude, with a questionable moral compass. Whether it's truly as leaderless as it purports to be is debatable. But could it be the first primitive manifestation of a new model of power and decision-making? At the time of this writing, Anonymous is predominantly made up of young white males. No wonder its nature reflects a young male's predilection for pranks, rebellion against authority, and cocky arrogance. As the tech-savvy Millennial generation ages and the internet becomes less and less the province of young white men, what might be the sensibilities of an internet "do-ocracy" made up of a broader swath of people? The optimist in me speculates: could this become the government of the future? No world wars, no charismatic leaders and dueling egos, not even a lot of debate or compromise, just large-scale, hive-mind movements to shut down the technology of whatever power structure isn't serving the collective good?

Speculation aside, compare this model, where the egoless minds of many combine to create a superior form of knowledge and direction for all—a kind of super-mind—to the more familiar hierarchical model where the intelligence of one extraordinary mind guides and influences many minds. The former is free of biases, power inequalities, personal agendas, self-aggrandizement, and even the financial costs that can accompany a single influence. What's more, it's capable of reaching a higher quality of wisdom than a single mind ever can. Though still in its infancy, this new form of intelligence has already begun to overshadow and replace any number of hierarchically organized industries.

Relating this new model to our journey here, the very act of reading a book is typically a hierarchical experience where the information of the book flows from author via the written word to the reader.

In *Holding a Butterfly*, and in these pages, readers are invited into a community of other readers to have a virtual experience together. I've heard many readers report having an intuitive sense of "being" with those others. One woman felt that she was being guided to give reassurance to a young, frightened pregnant woman. Another reader, a healer, felt guided to reach out through time and space to help someone heal a broken arm. Made-up stories or real meetings in the One Mind? We will probably never know but, still, readers have these profound experiences of and with others far beyond me. This is an example of a book moving from the traditional hierarchical experience to a lateral, peer-to-peer one.

In the early 2000s, a second generation of the World Wide Web evolved, referred to as Web 2.0, where a shift in emphasis occurred from the passive viewing of static website content to more dynamic, interactive uses that require a community of users to function and create community through their use (think Facebook). What we're exploring here through this book is a kind of Metaphysics 2.0—a second generation of consciousness-based personal growth practices that shift the emphasis from single practitioners interacting with static content and exercises to interactive practices requiring and creating virtual communities in consciousness. Just as Web 2.0 has given rise to broad scale collaboration and sharing among virtual online communities, this second generation of spiritual practices gives rise to connectivity and synergy among virtual communities in consciousness via the One Mind. I suspect this is of far greater benefit than anything I, as an author and teacher, might have to say.

Ultimately, I can imagine that this direct, peer-to-peer experience in the One Mind, where the power of the collective is the catalyst and change agent for healing, manifestation and wisdom, will diminish our dependence upon teachers, healers, and spiritual leaders as well as the importance of specific techniques, dogma, or rituals. As is happening in so many other contexts, the power is in all of us together rather than in any one person or any vehicle beyond the power of our own consciousness to connect us to the One Mind—and by "One Mind," of course, I'm referring to the universal, etheric web of connection rather than the technological one.

Exposure to One Mind experiences can't help but evolve our whole sense of who and what we are. The long-held understanding of humans as being separate entities holding separate, finite quantities of knowledge is eroding, and this in turn is eroding old hierarchical lines of power and dissemination. An isolated individual seeking information must go to another individual or group of individuals possessing separate knowledge pools. Twenty years ago, when I wanted to research something, I went to the library and found the wisdom of a handful of minds. Now I simply look things up online and, in just moments, find relevant information from a huge and diverse range of minds. Similarly, where once we may have needed teachers or priests as a pathway to higher knowledge, perhaps now we're more ready, willing and able to connect directly to the One Mind for wisdom, inspiration, knowledge, healing and empowerment.

Spiritual practices designed to elicit transcendent states are nothing new. What is new is the amplified field of consciousness created through the attention and intention of all of us together. This field offers an easy path of access to the One Mind and doesn't require a lifetime of disciplined practice in order to connect.

This isn't a push to bypass the work of spiritual maturity with quick short cuts. Aiming for spiritual awakening before we've prioritized personal maturation is a bit like turning on the light in a dark room and staring at the bare bulb in fascination until we're blinded. With maturity, turning on the light isn't about the phenomenon of the bulb; its purpose is to become more effective through all we can now see.

The exercises here are to help you become more effective in your world and, should you find yourself becoming less functional in your everyday life through practicing them, then this work is not for you. At the same time, I'm suggesting that in this era of fast-paced evolution, some things have shifted, in much the same way that what used to take a day at the library can now be accomplished in thirty minutes online. All of us together open portals that simply weren't available before.

Many of the anecdotes Dossey shares in *One Mind* describe individuals having extraordinary but unintentional experiences of feeling completely blended with another person, or at one with all life, or of their consciousness separating from their bodies. These experiences give dramatic illustrations of the One Mind but are far from the everyday that most of us inhabit. Yet there are many everyday pathways into the extraordinary. Perhaps the most accessible pathway of all into One Mind experience is through love and compassionate empathy where we intentionally extend our willingness to care for and identify with another—the experience most at the core of our exercises here.

Another pathway that we've also explored here in depth is imagination. Power-of-intention teachings emphasize the importance of focused imagining because imagination can take us to places we've never been. It can bypass the need for belief, it's the beginning of the creative process, and it's a powerful doorway into intuition and other One Mind experiences. What sometimes feels like our imagination making up a story can easily carry us beyond the limits of our small mind into the One Mind where we connect telepathically with other beings, access universal wisdom, have experience outside of linear time, and tap energy resources for healing and manifestation.

The next exercise is a dip into the One Mind through the vehicle of imagination. For this experiment, first identify an important question, concern, or area of life where you could best use wise guidance.

If you could meet with the world's wisest counselor for advice, what would you ask? This might relate to a pressing need for healing, an issue needing clarity, or guidance related to something new you want to create or call into your life. Choose whatever feels most pressing, important, and emotionally charged. As something comes to mind, write it down; this will give added clarity, intention and energy to your concern.

Exercise: Tapping the One Mind

Part I

Begin by bringing to mind someone who is a special teacher to you. This could be a person you know personally or someone you only know through their work such as an author, world leader, or historical figure. It could be someone either living or dead. Take some quiet, uninterrupted time for the following. Have writing materials close at hand to record your experiences. You may ritualize this if you wish with background music and by lighting a candle to represent the highest qualities of this individual.

Meditation

Quiet your mind for a moment and let your attention float free. Take a deep breath or two to help you transition to a soft, open mental state...

Let your sense of identification shift from the density and limitation of matter to a bright, clear, beautiful energy that is your true essence. As you make this shift in perception you leave behind the limitations of dense matter and start to see the cells of your physical body lighting up and becoming radiant with this energy... And now, all the particles that make up your body are becoming lighter; the molecules, the atoms, the sub-atomic particles all spreading out, vibrating in beautiful light.

Picture the bright energy of everyone in this miracle experiment network of souls, past, present and future, vibrating together in joined consciousness beyond the illusionary limits of space and time. Each of us is bringing our highest and best to whole. As a group we form a powerful network for healing and miracles. Our joined intentions quicken our growth, awaken our intuition and heighten our magnetism to our highest good. What has seemed difficult in the past will come more easily now. Together we open a portal to the One Mind that now streams the light of wisdom to each of us...

Bring to mind the person you picked as a special teacher. If you find yourself unexpectedly thinking of someone else instead, trust this new direction. Your intuition may guide you to a different teacher for a reason.

Think of the best and highest in this teacher, all the qualities you most admire. Open your heart in love for this person, feeling an overflowing of gratitude for all that you've received. Even if this is someone you've never met, know that their light has touched you all the same or they wouldn't be in your mind now, and be grateful.

As you offer the unconditional love of gratitude, love that's free of personal agendas and not needing anything in return, you see their light growing even brighter. When we see and love the best in another we naturally connect with their best and draw it forth. Your love helps your teacher to have more resources with which to assist you. You have created a bond in the One Mind.

Imagine this person's Higher Self now coming to you with a message or gift. At the level of our Higher Selves we're all part of One Mind and joined in love, so whether or not you've ever met this person, trust that he or she is here out of deep love for you. Know that you are truly in the presence of this being's soul, even though it may feel that you're making it up. Imagination is a potent doorway into intuition. As you visit with this being in your imagination, he or she may speak to you, sharing information, reassurance, or guidance. Your teacher may show you something or simply radiate love and healing. If you have formulated a specific question, ask it now and allow this other to respond.

If it's difficult to imagine words or images, simply think of your teacher now transmitting to you a wave of energy. Imagine this energy flowing into your head, being received by your higher mind as ideas that will become conscious in time. Feel it being received by your heart as pure love. Imagine your energy blending with that of your teacher so that your whole being absorbs this transmission of love and wisdom, turning it into whatever you most need for your growth at this time.

Now imagine yourself in the role of your teacher, seeing yourself from your teacher's view. From this perspective, counsel yourself, imagining what your teacher would say. Offer wisdom, healing, and whatever gifts are most needed. Write down the messages you receive.

When you feel complete with your visit, sit in gratitude for a moment and then return your attention to your body and your surroundings. Come back feeling refreshed and alert.

Part II

While it's easy to imagine a favorite mentor as having the gifts we most
need, that isn't the end of this exercise. The truth is that everyone is a
spiritual being of profound complexity, wisdom, and depth. Every being
has important gifts to offer us. This includes our friends, family
members, coworkers, complete strangers, and even the people we don't
like. The more we're willing to believe this and seek it out, the more we'll
find it. What we see in others, we tend to call forth, whether it's their
highest or lowest behavior. Believing in the goodness and wisdom of
others is the key that unlocks a flow of riches from people who didn't
even know, themselves, that they had it to give. The transmission of
spiritual gifts doesn't happen at the personality level. It happens when we
stop being hooked by all the dramas and dances that are so compelling to
our personalities and that limit our experience of love. It happens when
we rise into the One Mind. The next part of this exercise might just
surprise you with a new and completely different perspective on your
situation.

On separate 3x5 cards, write the names of at least a dozen people. Start
with at least several people you respect and admire. As with the last
exercise, these can be people whom you know personally or by
reputation. Next, include an equal number of people from your closest
peer and family relationships, such as your spouse, close friends, parents
or children, etc. Also include an equal number of people who are
acquaintances: coworkers, neighbors, etc. Finally, include an equal
number of people from your least-liked list, the people who annoy you,
who have hurt you, those whom you judge or feel judged by, public
figures you dislike, etc.

When you've completed this card deck full of names, shuffle the cards
together and place them face down in front of you. Hold your important
question in mind and randomly pick one card from the pile, trusting that
this is someone who has an important perspective to offer you. Read

through the previous exercise, only this time substitute the person whose card you picked.

If this turns out to be someone you know well, give special attention to seeing past the personality you've become so familiar with to perceive the rich, multifaceted spiritual being that shines through but is not limited to the body and personality you know. Realize this being to be wise, loving, and powerful beyond anything you've experienced in your personal relationship.

If the person who came up is someone you don't like, it might seem that this is the last person who would ever have gifts for you. You may need to take extra time coming into a state of love and gratitude, but imagine that it will be worth the effort. Recognize that as you are willing to imagine the highest in this individual, you also call it forth, so approach this with the willingness to step beyond the love-denying energy field you have created between you. Imagine that even this soul has important wisdom, guidance, healing, and love for you. As you imagine yourself in this other's role offering counsel, don't be surprised if you receive a surprisingly different view with a new perspective worth considering.

※※※※※

This is an exercise you may choose to expand upon and revisit from time to time. Add new people to your deck as it feels right to do so and randomly choose one or more voices from the stack whenever you'd like a fresh perspective. The more you practice in this way, the more you will hone your intuitive skills and ability to tap the great resource of the One Mind.

Chapter 12: Beyond Time and Space

The research on time is truly mind-bending. As Lynne McTaggart put it in her book, *The Intention Experiment*, "The central problems of going 'back to the future' and manipulating our own past are the logical knots the mind gets tied up in when considering them."[1] Reviewing just a fraction of the large body of science on time, she concluded that, "physicists no longer consider retrocausation [that is, changing the past] inconsistent with the laws of the universe." She went on to say that more than one hundred articles in scientific literature suggest various ways in which the laws of physics can account for time displacement.

Increasingly, we're seeing that time as a line doesn't really exist at all. How this affects our work here is that it shortcuts a lot of the rules of popular practices that assume we must perform a series of steps in order to see results, as in: read the book, practice the exercises, see results. Or: change your beliefs, change your mind, and then see results.

It's crazy to think it could happen in any other order, right? But when we free our minds from the "logical knots" that make all forms of retrocausation seem absurd, and allow ourselves to be imaginative enough to think beyond linear time, vast new possibilities open up. We might experience a result before we've practiced any steps or even opened the book, by way of an intention or state of consciousness we will hold in the future and send back in time to ourselves. Sometimes going step by step in a logical, linear progression is what we most need in order to assimilate change. But now it's not the only possibility.

When I teach classes on this material, I often have people come up to me with interesting stories of synchronicities and fortunate coincidences that occurred as soon as they bought my book but before they read it. Or they might come up to me right after I've led an exercise in sending intention back in time, and share their strong intuition of a past event they believed was affected by what we just did in the class.

And, of course, these anecdotes are much harder to track than when wonderful results come serendipitously *after* doing an exercise, but I do have one story that offers a compelling example of sending consciousness through time. It's a story I received from someone reading *Holding a Butterfly*.

He said that he woke up with such a bad sore throat and swollen tonsils that he made a doctor's appointment for that day. But in the afternoon, it quickly got better, and he cancelled his appointment. The next morning, he awoke with a slight touch of it back and sat down for his morning meditation.

My book was nearby and he randomly opened it to the chapter entitled '*Healing a condition at its start.*' He said he was pleased but not gob smacked by the synchronicity of opening to just the chapter he needed, but he was far more astonished as he read into the exercise that guided him to send health back in time to himself to 2 p.m. in the past, which is about when he suddenly improved the day before.

With the rise in popularity of power-of-intention teachings, collectively we've been working on assimilating the truth that consciousness alone can change our physical circumstances, and this is stretching our collective understanding of reality beyond a purely mechanical universe.

To put this in simple terms, our collective acceptance of the idea that if we physically push on something it will move is expanding to include the possibility that if we hold a conscious intention, we may see something physical move.

These teachings have prepared us to start the assimilation of an even broader understanding of the nature of reality as being nonlinear and not limited by the linear parameters of time. So, in other words, the new acceptance that we can hold an intention and see things move can now begin to expand to include the possibility that things may shift now as a result of an intention we hold tomorrow.

This dimension of working outside of time becomes even more powerful when we join it with the amplification of group intention, as we are in these exercises. This creates a dynamic that can propel an individual beyond the limitations of their own doubts, fears and lack of faith to experience truly miraculous outcomes.

As I've worked quite a bit with healing and healers over the years, I've been particularly interested in how healing might be approached outside of time. Consider the difference between aiming healing intention at a well-established illness in the present or aiming healing at the root beginnings of an illness when it was barely there.

Or how about aiming it right at the very moment a shift was made from health to dis-ease? As the early indications of research on sending intention back in time suggest, healing energy may actually be more effective outside of time.[2]

Psychologist William Braud, who has amassed the largest body of research demonstrating that human intention can affect not just inanimate objects but other living organisms, suggests that there might exist "seed" moments, perhaps at the onset of a condition, where the past is more readily changed. His research led him to believe that time-displaced healing intention (healing sent back to heal a condition in the past) might actually be more effective than real time healing methods. [3]

One problem, however, with concentrating on simply disappearing a physical symptom in the present or the past is that, in my experience, illness is highly purposeful. It results when we've somehow grown out of alignment with our highest good and highest purpose. Whether it's on the small scale of several days in bed with the flu or years of struggle with a debilitating illness, getting sick has a wonderful way of stopping us in our tracks, forcing us into new priorities, and redirecting our lives. From the big-picture paradigm of our Higher Self, illness helps satisfy un-met needs and gets us back on track in ways our conscious choices don't. Sometimes this is as simple as a few days of enforced rest when we're feeling overwhelmed and need a little assimilation time. A more serious illness may push us to change a lifetime's worth of old habits or tap strengths and resources we would never access without the crisis. Remember the words by Bruce Lipton I quoted in an earlier chapter: "Crisis ignites evolution." Even though we may address any number of symptoms, the root of an illness won't go away until we willingly choose the new priorities ill health forces upon us. When we ignore our minor symptoms, we tend to invite "louder" ones.

I first learned this from one of my early teachers of energetic healing. She was very gifted and had seen any number of spontaneous healings happen in her work with people. She shared one of her most significant lessons related to focusing simply on making a symptom go away. An avid cyclist came to her with a pained knee that was keeping him from the long hours of competitive cycling that he loved. She put all of her will into fixing his knee and in a single session, both healer and recipient felt the dramatic shift of an instantaneous healing. The man went away thrilled to have his knee completely cured and she was quite proud of herself. He got right back to cycling obsessively and in a short amount of time came back to her with a broken leg. This time she understood that "healing" him wasn't about fixing the injury; it was about quieting the soul that couldn't bear to sit still for even a moment. Her work with him then transitioned into helping him discern what his body was telling him and what growth could be found in the stillness that wasn't to be found in the comfort zone of endless cycling. Our greatest strengths, when we over-use them and have learned all we can from them, eventually can become weaknesses when our Higher Self is ready to learn something new, and this can create vulnerabilities in our physical health.

Presuming that we call in challenging situations to learn lessons, to develop new priorities as a personality and greater maturity as a soul, we won't just send healing back into the past in our exercise here. Instead, this easy healing process begins by mentally accessing a point in the past, before the seed moment of choosing illness, where the body has no experience of the dis-ease—a time where there is a cellular memory of vibrant health. This is just the starting place, however, because this state of pre-disease is essentially an immature state. If dis-ease is part of a growth process, the state prior to it may lack symptoms but it also lacks the spiritual growth, wisdom and maturity that come with the discomfort.

So, the next step in this process is to imagine into a future time where the lessons of the dis-ease have been learned; where maturity and wholeness have been achieved. It doesn't matter where in time this is—and it's not necessary to figure out when this will occur or even to believe there is such a point. The exercise only requires imagining it. You don't even need to understand whether or not this point of wholeness is achieved within the context of your current life-time. When you are able to imagine an early state of health and a future state of wholeness, the next step is to mentally bring these two states together and collapse the time in between, bypassing the illness altogether.

The process of this is very simple, yet the growth that this kind of intention sets in motion is far-reaching. Energy follows intention and we're setting in motion a very different intention than that of simply disappearing an illness. Essentially, what we're doing here involves renegotiating soul choices. Invariably, any condition that we struggle with has gains along with the pain.

To accept right now the wisdom and maturity of an evolved state means accepting a speeded up growth track that may well take us beyond the comfort zone of what's familiar. Another element here that makes this work particularly powerful is the aspect of group energy. As we hold the intention to claim our health and wholeness in the context of this amplifying power of all of us together, it may happen more quickly than we expect. In *Holding a Butterfly*, I wrote in depth on the responsibility that comes with growth and empowerment, and the reasons we might choose to resist these:

> *Awakening power can be accomplished simply through the slightest act of intention and may offer little evidence, immediately, that anything at all is different. Yet this intentional willingness to become more fully our True Self opens the door for God's Will to override our plans, taking us in directions we may never have anticipated. What began imperceptibly takes on a life of its own and may change us dramatically, sometimes in ways that feel unexpected and out of control since our ego is no longer leading the way. Yet the journey is always in the direction of our highest good and highest joy.*[4]

These soul choices of healing into wholeness aren't necessarily ones we can comprehend or make from the limited vision of our personalities, so we will approach this in a way that respects its complexity. We will create the pathway and opportunity for profound transformation to occur and then hand it over to Higher Wisdom, rather than our personal will, to determine the perfect pace for this process.

But first it's important to address the resistance that often arises at the whole notion that illness is purposeful and somehow connected to "choice." It understandably causes many to bristle because of how easily it can be distorted into a form of "blaming the victim." So, before moving into the miracle experiment at the end of this chapter, a deeper exploration of the complicated nature of this principle and how it can facilitate self-healing, is in order.

There are many proponents of mind-body healing who hold that we're responsible for the health or illness of our physical body only to a point and then heredity, circumstance, and environmental factors kick in. However, when we take a longer, spiritual view, and let go of the assumption that illness is bad, or that we must have done something wrong to bring it upon us, any illness can be seen as purposeful, both to the personality and to the soul.

The ego—the part of us that believes we're defined by the limits of our physical body and, thus, highly vulnerable—can't help but find illness threatening and regard it as the enemy. The ego tries to "control" its way to safety. Consequently, the idea that our circumstances are connected to our state of consciousness simply motivates the ego to exercise greater self-control, with illness being a sign of failure.

But, we can only control what's within the range of our conscious awareness. Illness is often a way we bring unconscious, non-integrated aspects of self to the surface so that we can open to new and better options. This is, perhaps, one of its most important functions. Rather than seeing illness as our failure to control our health, it's more useful to view it as a sign that we're ready to grow.

No one consciously chooses pain or disease—it's not something we have done "wrong"—yet the experience of dealing with these challenges can lead us on a journey that ultimately delivers great rewards. I've heard many people with cancer and other life-threatening diseases describe their illness as one of the greatest blessings of their lives because it forced them to completely reshuffle priorities and pursue new paths that brought profound fulfillment. The illness gave them permission to make choices they wouldn't have considered otherwise.

If you find yourself skeptical of this premise, ask yourself, if faced with a serious or minor illness, would you rather feel yourself to be a helpless victim at the mercy of it or an engaged student learning from it? Which state of mind do you think would best serve your healing process and your peace of mind? There is no right or better answer to these questions. If it feels punishing to look at your disease this way, then this material won't serve you and you may want to skip to the next chapter. If, on the other hand, it feels empowering to discover a meaning to your symptoms, read on.

What Are Your Symptoms Telling You?

Even at times we don't consider ourselves ill, we may still have a symptom or two: chronic allergies, a tendency toward headaches, a pain or weakness in a particular body part, or a susceptibility to certain kinds of illness. Whether we're dealing with the experience of serious illness or simply the occasional minor symptom, listening to these physical manifestations of dis-ease can uncover levels of meaning and purposefulness that we may never have realized were there.

Our physical symptoms communicate to us in a language filled with obvious metaphors. If we're willing to pay attention, they tell us a great deal about our needs, our imbalances, and our path of healing. The very metaphors we use in speaking often mirror the physical symptoms our body manifests. I first became aware of this when I was director of a Center for Attitudinal Healing in Baltimore, MD and worked extensively with people dealing with physical illnesses. I noticed how people's pet expressions had a way of literally describing their illness. A woman with cancerous tumors in her leg frequently used the expression, "I can't stand it!" Someone with food allergies often said, "I can't stomach it!" A woman with skin cancer spoke of things "getting under her skin." (As I shared these examples in a workshop once, a woman spoke up and said, "I have difficulty receiving from people, and I just realized that my favorite expression is, 'I can't take it!'")

To start understanding the language of your own physical symptoms, consider the metaphorical meanings of the affected body parts and functions. For example, hands are for handling things. If you have pain in your hands, ask yourself: are you are holding on too tightly in some way? Are you trying to "handle" everything yourself? Do you have difficulty "reaching out" for love and support? Are you having difficulty "grasping" something? If your neck and shoulders hurt, are you "shouldering" more than your share of responsibility? Are you being "stiff-necked," or overly rigid in how you're seeing things? If you are a woman with tumors or pain in your breasts, have you been suckling the world until there's nothing left for you? Do you feel in need of nurturing yourself? Do you feel in some way inadequate about yourself as a woman? If you have heart problems, have you felt "heartbroken?" Have you closed your heart to warmth and love? Have you lost your joy and passion for life? See which metaphors best fit the way you feel.

A woman in one of my workshops couldn't see how there could be any link between the back injury she sustained in a car accident (that was in no way her fault) and her emotional needs until I asked how easy or difficult it was for her to feel supported in life and to allow others to support her. (Our spine is what provides "support.") She admitted that receiving support had always been extremely difficult for her. As a result of the injury, however, her life changed to include a regular routine of various therapies with caring professionals whose sole agenda was to "support" her.

Addressing the situation indicated by the metaphor can powerfully assist healing and sometimes even alleviate the need for other treatment. For example, during a time when I felt sorely burdened by the pressures of life ("shouldering" more than I could carry, so to speak) I developed a painful frozen shoulder condition for which a medical professional prescribed several months of certain-to-be-painful physical therapy. Before going this route, I "treated" my emotional condition of feeling burdened by clearing many projects from my plate and giving myself a highly uncharacteristic, several-month break. I played more, worked less, and made relaxing a priority. As I felt less stressed, my shoulder improved so quickly that I wound up not needing the physical therapy.

In recounting my own experience, I don't mean to encourage anyone to forgo sensible medical supervision or suffer unnecessarily. I am suggesting, however, that we not rely solely on medicine to effect healing. Listening to our symptoms and letting them guide us somewhere instead of seeking the most passive release from discomfort isn't the easiest path in the short term, but it invariably holds the richest rewards in the long term, and it creates a strong foundation for conventional medical treatments to be successful.

While there are some amazingly literal connections that can be made between symptoms and illnesses, it's also important to recognize that there's no simple mind-body cookbook explanation that can be applied to every illness. There may be profound spiritual purposes to a condition that aren't readily visible. For example, my dear friend, Cheryl, born with a crippling degenerative disease that took her life when she was thirty-one, was occasionally accosted by overly-eager healers who told her that if she only had enough faith, she could heal. She took offense at this, primarily because these individuals assumed that just because she lived life in a wheelchair and in an obviously different body, that she was not "healed." Cheryl strongly believed there to be a spiritual purpose for her physical disability and that she had, at some deep soul level, "chosen" it to help her learn to love life no matter what. She felt her life lesson was not to change her physical body but to appreciate life in spite of any pain and limitation her body created. By the end of her life, she unquestionably did.

Many people are familiar with Louise Hay's classic book, *You Can Heal Your Life*, with its listing of physical symptoms and their corresponding emotional dynamics. While I highly recommend this as a useful reference to have on hand, I don't suggest you start by reading someone else's interpretation of your symptoms.

Symptoms and their messages are complex and very personal. Sometimes reading what the expert has to say closes our minds to our own insights and even if a correspondence is right on the money for us, if we don't feel the truth of it for ourselves, the information won't change anything.

In coming to an understanding of why we have a particular symptom, instead of rushing quickly to a neat and tidy theory about what it means, it's perhaps enough, at first, to simply trust that there is meaning, maybe many layers of meaning. While the following exercise offer some insight into the language of physical symptoms, keep in mind that a dis-ease often speaks to us on many levels at once. Be mindful not to latch on to one explanation to the exclusion of all others. Keep listening and opening, letting the messages of your body take you deeper into "Self" understanding.

Exercise: The Language of Symptoms

Step One

- Where in your body do you manifest physical symptoms?
- What chronic or recurring physical conditions do you have?

Step Two

What are all the physical functions of this part of the body and what metaphors come to mind related to these functions? Also look at some of your pet expressions and see if they have physical body references. These expressions may tell you something about real symptoms you manifest. For example, from childhood well into adulthood, I used to be prone to headaches. An expression I used to say frequently was, "I feel like my head's going to explode!" I didn't say this when I had a headache, when I literally did feel like my head would explode. Instead, this was my spontaneous expression of exasperation when I had too many things going on in my life and in my mind, and felt overwhelmed. Play and free associate with your own metaphors and expressions until they reveal insights into the emotional dynamics underlying your symptoms. Needless to say, if you discover such an expression in your own vocabulary, remove it so that you don't continue to inadvertently affirm it as a literal physical condition.

Step Three

Next, ask yourself how this physical condition might be serving you. For example, I discovered over the years that headaches had a number of payoffs for me. One thing it did was to slow my mind down when I felt overwhelmed. When my head was full of pain, it wasn't full of thoughts. Also, after noticing that I would sometimes get a migraine after several days of feeling particularly happy, I became aware that happiness didn't feel safe to me. Growing up in an alcoholic family included frequent disappointments, and feeling happy and hopeful was often followed by an unforeseen disappointment shaking my world. This childhood experience left me feeling undefended and frightened when my spirits lifted too high for too long. A headache brought me back down to earth where, even though I felt unhappy, at least I wasn't worrying about how far I'd fall when the next disappointment struck. I wasn't conscious that I was doing this—it certainly wasn't an intentional choice to be in physical pain. Shutting down high emotions, be they of overwhelm or of happiness, was an automatic response I learned in childhood as a protective mechanism.

I had this revelation one day as I walked around a Minneapolis lake (with a migraine) and, for the remainder of my walk, I imagined the feeling of being strong coexisting in my body with the feeling of being happy. Holding these two experiences at once felt very foreign. Happiness had feelings of vulnerability intertwined in it and strength didn't feel at all happy. It took a bit of practice to imagine feeling strong and happy at the same time, but by the end of my walk, I could do it. I stopped having frequent migraines after this. They didn't subside gradually, they just stopped, so, instead of suffering through a migraine every week or two, I went for many months without a single headache. Now headaches are rare occurrences and when I have them, they are far less severe.

So, ask yourself what your physical symptom may be helping you, allowing you, or forcing you to do, be, or have that you wouldn't otherwise experience. Consider even those things you wouldn't normally define as positive. Specifically:

- Is it forcing you to let others help you?

- Is it causing you to spend your time differently? If so, what might be the gain in this?

- Are you receiving attention (positive or negative) that you wouldn't otherwise get? If so, how is that attention giving you something you need or expect? (Sometimes negative attention preserves a familiar identity we're not ready to let go of, or keeps people from expecting too much from us, to name just a couple of possible gains.) Was illness the way you received love and attention when you were young?

- Is your illness resulting in your developing new strengths and resources?

- Is it preserving a familiar identity? If so, what is that identity and what might you lose that you don't want to lose if you acted outside your own box?

- It is allowing you to put off doing something burdensome or frightening?

- Is it protecting you from failing by preventing you from beginning something?

- Does it distract you and keep your attention away from things that are too painful to look at? Does physical pain take the place of emotional pain?

- Does it allow you to avoid painful or frightening emotions, such as anger, sadness, guilt, or shame? Is illness a way you implode instead of explode?

- Does it give you permission to say "No," set boundaries, get angry, be selfish, or grieve?

- How are your relationships with others affected by your symptom? Have they deepened as a result? Does it provide an acceptable way to be vulnerable and more open emotionally? Does it create "space" interpersonally: fewer relationships, more privacy, or more time alone? Does this condition offer protection from intimacy and possible hurts that could result from getting close?

Step Four

If you were able to identify any secondary gains that your symptoms hold for you, what would you need to do to receive these gains without needing the physical condition? The true answer to this question invariably involves stepping away from familiar behavior and often has a "wrong" feeling to it initially, as healing may require going against deeply ingrained conditioning.

It might mean giving yourself a day off without being sick first, or finding ways to ask for (and feel entitled to) the love, attention and support you crave without having to "need" it because you're sick. If we look deeply enough into the payoffs of our illnesses we're likely to uncover ways that our lifestyle has gotten off track. We may find that we have devoted so much energy to doing what we believe we should that we've neglected what we truly want. While this may push us toward difficult choices, the end results are far richer than simply being symptom-free.

⟐⟐⟐⟐⟐⟐⟐

Living with a Life-Threatening Illness

If you are currently living with a life-threatening illness, consider replacing the question, "How can I get well?" with the questions "What do I want to get well for? What do I want to live for? Do I feel complete with my life as it stands? If not, what is there left for me to do?" True healing occurs when we embrace our passion and purpose for living rather than our battle with illness and fear of death. This means living as though each day is our last, completing whatever is unfinished and making the most of each moment. When we pursue healing in this way, the outcome of the disease becomes less important. We may find that our physical healing process speeds up miraculously, or that our symptoms remain the same but no longer inhibit our joy in living. We may find that our disease progresses, yet we experience a profound sense of peace around the transition of death. When we live every day this way, ultimately we call forth whatever outcome best serves our highest good, and we feel at peace with it.

Illness and Children

This look at healing would be incomplete without some mention of how the principles discussed here apply when children get sick. Are the same principles even relevant? Our human instinct is to shield our children from suffering to the very best of our ability. This very human truth makes it challenging to see past it to the spiritual truth that what dies out of the human condition lives on in spirit, with the pain and damage of the physical realm ultimately passing into illusion. Both of these human and spiritual truths need to be honored.

While it is heartbreaking for all involved when a child becomes sick, suffers, and dies, if we look at this situation from a spiritual perspective, there are certain to be profound lessons and gifts that each family member receives through such a life-changing experience. These lessons may never be apparent to an observer.

Elizabeth Kubler Ross, author of the groundbreaking book, *On Death and Dying*, noticed in her work with dying children that their spiritual development is far greater than that of healthy children. Could it be that a child who dies is a highly evolved soul who chooses to engage with and influence a group of souls on a physical level but would not be served by a longer experience in this physical reality? I have no definitive answers here, just a suggestion to let go of your certainties around illness, healing and death; then see where your mind is able to go.

Miracle Experiment: Healing Outside of Time

Before reading into the next experiment, identify your most important desire for healing. This could be physical or emotional in nature. It could be a repeating pattern such as a tendency to be in crisis around money or to feel unloved.

When you've identified what is most important to you at this time, imagine for a moment that there are unknown thousands of people from the past and future who have given you their loving attention and intention. This may have already changed your life. Let any knots in your mind relax around this and just enjoy the uncertainty and mystery of uncharted possibilities...

Meditation

Relax your body and quiet your thoughts with some deep, slow breaths...

See the bright energy of everyone in this miracle experiment network of souls joining you. All of us are once again vibrating together in joined consciousness beyond the illusionary limits of space and time, each of us bringing only higher love to the whole. See this joining as beautiful, sacred, awe-inspiring, and filled with the potent energy of love. As a group we form a powerful network for healing and miracles.

Let your sense of identification start to shift from the density and limitation of matter to a bright, clear, beautiful energy that is your true essence. As you make this shift in perception you leave behind the limitations of dense matter and start to see the cells of your physical body lighting up and becoming radiant with this energy... All the particles that make up your body are becoming lighter; the molecules, the atoms, the sub-atomic particles, all spreading out, vibrating in beautiful light. As you leave the density of matter behind, you enter a realm of limitless possibilities where time and space have no bearing.

Now bring to mind the experience of dis-ease that you would like to release. Gently hold it in the light of possibility, without even quite knowing what this means... If it's a condition that has weighed you down, imagine it transforming, for the moment, into something light that you can hold in your hand as lightly as you would a butterfly. Then let it easily fly away.

Now, in your imagination, feel back in time to a point of wellness, before there was any trace of dis-ease. You don't need to see any specific information about when this point in time is. It's more important to feel it; to recall in your body an experience of vitality, health and well-being. If it's hard to imagine that there was such a time in this life, go back even further, before your consciousness came into this body, until you find a place where you are fresh and new, full of health and innocence. Notice how this experience of newness feels as pure sensation in your body. Bring it to life in your imagination and take a moment to enjoy it...

Now, feel into the future to a point where you have either released this dis-ease or have evolved to a place where you no longer suffer and it no longer impedes your well-being. You don't need to know when in time this is. Just trust that there is such a point and see what it feels like. It could be soon; it could be many years from now; it could be beyond your current physical life-time. It doesn't matter where it is. You don't even have to believe there will be such a point. Just imagine what it would feel like if there were. It's okay if you feel like you're making it all up.

Imagine that the experience of this dis-ease matured you in some way. It may have taught you any number of lessons: to be strong, or to show your vulnerability; to be compassionate or to reach out for help; to tap your depths or to awaken gifts of healing or creativity. From your perspective of being beyond it now, how do you see that you've grown from this experience of dis-ease?

Even if you don't immediately understand how you benefitted from this experience, trust that it opened new paths and tempered your personality and soul in important ways. From your perspective of maturity, you have the quiet confidence and strength that comes from knowing you are never a victim of your circumstances. You are at peace with all that has been and all that is. Notice what a gentle and easy sensation peace creates in your body and just relax into it...

Now, again, recall the earlier experience of fresh, vibrant health. Call it up clearly enough to feel the pleasure of it. Relax into it and let it bring a smile to your face... Imagine taking this pleasurable experience of health and holding it in your left hand...

Next, bring to mind the experience of peace, maturity and wholeness. Bring it to mind vividly enough that you can feel the very different kind of pleasure that comes with confidence, strength and peace. Relax into this state until it, too, brings a smile to your face... Now take this state of wholeness and imagine holding it in your right hand. See if you can feel the pleasurable states of vibrant health and mature wholeness at the same time...

Become aware of your two hands, each holding a different state, one from the past and one from the future. For the time being just allow the feeling in both of your hands to expand. At the end of this exercise, you will be given the chance to bring them together in a life-changing way, collapsing the time in between, by laying your two hands together over your heart.

If you decide to bring together the two realities you hold in your hands, it will set in motion the alchemy of transformation, speeding up your growth, removing your ego's resistance to God's love and putting you on a path of Divine Will. And then anything can happen. Your life becomes far less subject to the limitations of natural law and your personal agendas. Miracles become not just possible, but natural.

With this path, the familiar may no longer be an option and the ego may feel less in control. Unforeseen joys take the place of comfortable predictability. But before you decide what to do, open your awareness to include the thousands of others in this miracle experiment network, past, present, and future, who are undertaking this healing work with you.

See that some of them have chosen not to move forward into the next step, but many of them are. You see many hands coming together over hearts, collapsing time. These individuals step into bold new life paths of wholeness, filled with purpose and joy. Their first act of service is to shine loving intention to you so that you have more than your own resources to draw upon in this work.

This step may or may not be one you're ready to take now. You may feel these two energies irresistibly coming together, your hands being pulled together. Alternately, you may feel resistance. Listen to and trust your instincts on this. If you feel unsure, simply relax, be at peace, and do nothing until you know. You can't make the wrong choice here.

If now is not the time to set off such a major life change, bring your hands together over your head, imagining the two energies forming a ball of light there, right above your head. Know that even if now is not the time to engage this alchemy of change, you've created a pathway that will activate itself when the time is right, be it minutes or years from now.

If you are ready, bring your hands together over your heart and for a moment feel yourself immersed in a golden light... Breathe... relax... experience... Feel the many hearts and minds who are with you now in your healing into wholeness and receive...

Your first act of service is to shine this golden light to every soul in the miracle experiment network. Feel with them as they receive this energy to be used now or held in reserve for the right time.

As you reach out to the many of us, imagine one soul who has a particularly dramatic effect as they collapse time. Picture them having a powerful healing experience as they also step into a highly accelerated path of growth. Feel with this person their excitement, their joy, their surprise... You also sense this person's newfound strength, zest for life and passionate purpose. Let your heart overflow with joy for this other and spend a moment in their world with them as they become an important agent of change for good.

Breathe... come back... be at peace.

◇◇◇◇◇◇◇◇

This is a process that can be used for facilitating healing for someone else, and, for those of you who are healers and struggle with empathically joining with people in their pain, this is a great way to use your empathy without it being to your detriment. Instead of empathically joining with someone's illness, feel back into their past state of physical health, then feel forward into their wholeness and maturity. Then in your mind, bring these two states together over their head. Here you're being empathic but only joining with states that are healthy. Essentially, this process bypasses the illness altogether.

Here are the steps if you would like to try this on someone else.

Healing Outside of Time

1. As with any healing interaction, the first step is to put yourself in a quiet, peaceful frame of mind and to step away from any attachment you may have to the recipient's outcome.

2. The facilitator then lays hands on the recipient's shoulders, holding an intention to be a channel for God/Zero Point energy. Open your heart and join with this person in compassion. Rather than giving attention to any presenting dis-ease, imagine that you

are helping to soften their resistance to God energy so they'll be open to the highest outcome, whatever that may be.

3.   Focusing on the person to be healed, in your imagination bypass the illness and feel back in time to a place of wellness, before they had the dis-ease. You may intuitively pick up on some specific details about this, but this isn't necessary—it could even be distracting. What's more important is to join with the person at an experiential level so that you feel for them the memory of wellness. Use all your empathic skills here to feel into a state when they felt healthy.

4.   Now imagine forward in time to a place where they have matured into a greater state of wholeness—to a time when they have learned from the experience of illness and no longer feel limited by it or in pain. It could be that the individual has physically healed from the illness or it could be that it's still present, but they've evolved spiritually to the point where there's no longer any experience of suffering. This could even be a time beyond this lifetime. You don't need to know any details about this moment from their future. You just need to feel into it so you have the emotional experience of their maturity that no longer needs the suffering of this dis-ease.

5.   Bring the energies of these two "selves"—the past self with the body-memory of wellness, and the future self with maturity and freedom from suffering—together above the head of the current time "self." You can use your hands to do this if it helps make the experience stronger for you, but you can also do it all in your mind. This combines the body-memories of wellness with the maturity and evolution that no longer needs the illness.

6.   Now, put your personal agendas to the side and mentally (not out loud) speak to the person's Higher Self and offer this as a

7. pathway out of suffering and into an accelerated path of growth. Then, energetically step back. Don't assume a "yes." The decision is not yours to make. This speeded-up path has consequences. This is about taking a quantum leap into maturity as opposed to a step-by-step path. It means taking on greater responsibility that comes with maturity and living without some of the advantages of being a less-abled person.

8. This is really all you need to do. If the recipient isn't ready for this, you may feel the two states resist one another and/or resist coming down into current time. But they will still be there as a resource for the individual to draw upon when ready—which could be in twenty years or in fifteen minutes. So, as healer, you need to really keep your personal agendas and assumptions out of it. Simply hold space for the highest outcome. If the recipient is ready to choose this accelerated path of healing, you may sense it in some way. You may have an intuitive awareness of time collapsing, bringing the past state of health and the future state of wholeness together into one unified energy over the recipient's head and of that energy then being irresistibly drawn down into the receiver's current time experience. But if you experience none of this, don't assume that nothing has happened!

9. In general, I suggest that it's better not to share details of this process and your intuitive impressions with the recipient as you may plant thoughts in their mind that override rather than support their will.

Chapter 13: New Prosperity

There are countless books, seminars and techniques available these days on how to make more money, from financial strategies to metaphysical techniques. Whether they teach the power of intention or more pragmatic investment strategies, they all emphasize how to separate ourselves from the collective experience to create our own personal wealth. Yet, the new trends are all about *having* a collective experience, not separating from it, and this is true of new prosperity as well.

The Great Recession lasted only from 2008-2009 but it was followed by a long, slow recovery. As we touched upon in the last chapter, when crisis or illness occurs at the personal level, there's always some spiritual lesson, purpose, or payoff to be gained. It ultimately takes us somewhere we needed to go in the way it forces us to choose differently.
Crisis at the collective level is just as purposeful, forcing us toward new values and habits. In this case, as the economy languished, sharing economies of free and low-cost goods flourished.

In 2017, in dramatic contrast to the growth of new, grassroots sharing economies, Donald Trump assembled the richest cabinet in American history, full of kingpins of mega-industries with flagrant conflicts of interest, promising to further escalate the consequences of unchecked, old-paradigm, hierarchical power. Could this be anything other than a great push toward grassroots change? "Grassroots," of course, means that the onus for change is fully in the hands of each of us.

So what exactly is the change we're being pushed toward? Perhaps the clearest vision of this can be seen in some of the broad trends and characteristics of the millennial generation. This generation has been deeply affected by the depressed economy and they are also the generation most shaped by the new energy of Unity consciousness. What's more, as the largest generation in Western history, they will be setting the trends for many years to come.

While stereotypes of this generation abound—not all of which are flattering—there are some general patterns emerging. Along with being fused to their technology, millennials are the most accepting generation of differences, be they of race, nation or gender. Their easy access to people all over the world has shaped them to identify more globally and less nationally than any other generation. Their aspirations lean more toward quality of life, valuing meaningful work over high salaries, experiences over material things, and healthy lifestyle over the "drugs, sex, and rock n roll" life glamorized by other youth generations. They show a tendency toward social concern, liberal politics and caring about others. Being a good steward of resources is more important than merely having and spending, and they are more comfortable with sharing than previous generations, favoring access over ownership.

Perhaps the higher purpose of the global financial slump that hit so hard and has receded so slowly is that it's forcing us all, with millennials leading the way, to discern what's truly important, to become good stewards of what we have, to rely on each other, to share, and to focus on what's available to us without money.

Along these lines, Jeremy Rifkin, in his book *The Zero Marginal Cost Society,* goes so far as to suggest that because of the connectivity of the internet and the rapid evolution of 3-D printing, we could be heading into an era where goods and services become nearly free and capitalism, as well as the scarcity and the greed that accompany it, become virtually obsolete. Rifkin, a brilliant futurist, economist and best-selling author, has been a political advisor to the European Union and the People's Republic of China on issues related to the economy, climate change, and energy security. He was instrumental in shaping Germany's transition to a low-carbon economy, and China's strategic acceptance of climate policy. He makes the point that the very word "collaborative" didn't even exist until the mid-twentieth century and its usage shot up from the late sixties on, paralleling the development of the computer and internet technology.

This new kind of economic paradigm, where the collaborative exchange of free or nearly free goods and services eclipses both capitalist and socialist systems, won't just change our relationship to money, it promises to fundamentally change who we are and the whole way we go about life. Rifkin writes, "…the pursuit of self-interest is being tempered by the pull of collaborative interests, and the traditional dream of rags to riches is being supplanted by a new dream of a sustainable quality of life." He foresees "…billions of people to be individually 'empowered.' But that empowerment is only achievable by one's participation in peer-to-peer networks…"[1] What Rifkin outlines in great detail is the already-in-progress, practical manifestation of a very possible, wide-scale, societal shift from scarcity to abundance—something that is still difficult to fathom.

In this era, creating prosperity is much less about having money and more about having a thriving life. The cancer that grew out of the eighties push to "have it all' has given rise to a new aspiration to "have it good," including purposefulness, happiness, wellbeing and love. Inherent in this "good" life is a deep awareness of our connection to and responsibility for the whole. More than ever before, prosperity in this era comes through cooperation, collaboration, community and interdependence rather than through personal advancement. If you wish to thrive in these times, an important starting place is to strengthen your connections to networks.

It's easy to see how "me" consciousness created the malaise of our world—we're bombarded with examples of the environment being exploited for financial gain, of profiteering banksters, polarized politicians, and international corporations that are sacrificing the common good for personal gain. But what might be harder to recognize are all the ways that "me" consciousness isn't the exclusive purview of billionaires and corporations—it's something that many of us take part in. And it's not just a matter of overt greed and malevolence. Its more subtle manifestations include all the ways we get so caught up in ourselves that we have nothing left for the world around us. It might look like depression that causes us to isolate, or being completely absorbed in our worries and survival fears, or becoming so busy with the demands of life that there's no attention left for kindness or caring. It might look like stubborn self-sufficiency that forgets that others might want to be there to help if we could just bring ourselves to reach out. It's easy to isolate and separate from helpful networks at the point when we need them most, yet the more we do, the more we unwittingly align with the old energy of breakdown.

2017 initiated a wave of historically large demonstrations, the overt purpose of these being to resist the agenda of a new president and administration. But their by-product might be even more important. One effect of this wide-scale organizing was a national resurgence of participation among a citizenry that had become apathetic to its governing. Another effect was the bringing together of masses of people in small groups to form friendships and communities.

In 2017, immediately following the twenty-nine-year "coming of age" point of the Harmonic Convergence, people in the United States started coming together in a big way, not just online, but face-to-face. In small, grassroots action groups, people were forming and strengthening just the kind of connections that are foundational to new prosperity.

To again quote Jeremy Rifkin, "empowerment is only achievable by one's participation in peer-to-peer networks." Not being part of a web of connection may be more related to money woes and worries than we may realize. At purely emotional and energetic levels, stress, depression and isolation do not produce the consciousness conducive to attracting prosperity.

Dr. Lewis Mehl-Madrona was interviewed on Thom Hartmann's worldwide radio show in 2008 when many were dealing with depression directly related to the financial crisis. The Native American psychiatrist and author of *Coyote Medicine* and other books blending Western medicine and traditional Native American teachings, said that antidepressants work slowly if they work at all. He went on to say, "...what works quickly are friends. What works quickly is exercise. And I think that friends will get you through times of no money much better than money will get you through times of no friends. And what I tell people is call everyone you know and invite them to a meeting. Get them to come to your house. If you don't have a house, go to their house. And get people together to talk about how to help each other feel better during these depressing times."[2]

Cultivating meaningful connections requires an investment of time, which in today's fast-paced world we sometimes believe we don't have, especially when we are still operating in the old mode of doing everything for ourselves, by ourselves. As a move toward greater prosperity, instead of focusing on your wealth and self-sufficiency, consider the richness of your personal community. What is your experience of interdependence? Who's there for you emotionally, spiritually and in times of need? Who's there when you celebrate? Who can you rely on? Who are you there for? If self-sufficiency has triumphed over interrelatedness in your life, consider giving your greatest resources, your time and caring, toward nurturing relationships. Find those people with whom you can give and receive; with whom you can accomplish more together than separately; those people you can have fun with without spending money; and be fully yourself. It may seem costly to find the time, and not relevant to the goal of prosperity at all, yet, in the long run, it may be the wisest investment of your life.

If you don't have a supportive community in your life, the opportunities for finding one have never been more plentiful. Just go online and explore. Meetup.com will help you connect with spiritual communities, support communities, and interest groups; Indivisible.org and Ourrevolution.com with political action groups; Nextdoor.com with neighbors; Match.com with potential romantic partners, and so on.

Another way to be prosperously connected is through sharing networks. There are many easy sharing networks to join. Nextdoor.com, for example, is a wide-scale social media network that connects people within a neighborhood and enables all kinds of win/win exchanges. Starting in the United States, Nextdoor has a goal to become global and has already begun to spread to the U.K. and other parts of Europe. You might also consider creating sharing opportunities for your friends. Facebook makes this very easy. Invite everyone to bring their best, no longer needed items to give away and share with each other. Donate all that's left.

Once upon a time, everyone on a street block owned and stored one of every item they needed, even items that were seldom used and often costly. Increasingly nowadays, neighbors are creating ways to share. Littlefreelibrary.org helps neighbors create free book exchanges; other sites help neighbors create tool-lending libraries, car-sharing and more, so that now everyone on a block doesn't need to buy, own and store in order to have access.

Having spent much of my life buying, owning and storing, I'm finding the new trend to be highly refreshing. Just in the last year I found the perfect dining room chairs that a neighbor was practically giving away even though they were expensive high-end furniture. They were given to her by a friend and she no longer needed them. I couldn't have found more perfect chairs if I had shopped every store in town and paid five times as much. I enjoyed the experience of meeting a neighbor and inheriting chairs with a history. I gave my old chairs to a just-married millennial couple who were equally pleased. The ease of receiving what I wanted made the letting go of what I could no longer use that much easier as well.

I first taught the spiritual principles of prosperity in the 1980s and I used to stress the importance of letting go of what we no longer needed, asking people to imagine how amazing it would be if, on a wide scale, people freely circulated to one another the stockpile of things they owned but didn't use or enjoy. Back then, this was a futuristic fantasy, but now, watching the free flow of goods and services in my neighborhood, I see it come to life. If this is all new territory for you, consider exploring the growing world of sharing.

Another important aspect of prosperity in this era is stewardship. Rather than focusing on how much money you have, look at whether or not you have been a good steward of your money. For example, in the last year:

- How have you used your money to enhance the quality of your life?
- Have you used your money to intentionally prosper someone else?
- Have you used your money to support something you believe in?

Good stewardship is a big part of the higher consciousness that attracts abundance and becoming a good steward of what we have is often the catalyst that attracts more. I suggest following the practices below for at least a month to cultivate this consciousness of stewardship. Do recognize, however, that "stewardship" is not the same as "frugality." Stewardship implies responsible use of a resource, letting it flow in a way that benefits the whole, neither wasting nor hoarding.

Exercise: Financial Stewardship

Every time you spend even a cent, ask: "Is this expenditure taking my life in the direction I want it to go? Is this expenditure enhancing the quality of my life, prospering someone I would like to see prosper, or supporting something I believe in?" If not, rethink spending your money in that way.

Exercise: Creating Abundance Without Money

If you've become highly dependent upon money for recreation, self-nurturing, self-esteem, or socializing, try challenging yourself to find ways of enjoying life that don't require money. This can be a fun challenge to do with a group. When the easy crutch of money is taken away, you may find that creativity skyrockets, relationships deepen, and you have surprisingly meaningful new experiences. Try this as a personal exercise for a month, or start a no-money gathering for your friends. You might be amazed at the new forms of abundance you discover this way.

⟡⟡⟡⟡⟡⟡⟡

There are so many power-of-intention teachings that emphasize manifesting money in abundant quantities. Does new-era prosperity mean we have to live with less? Not necessarily. Teachings of old are correct in their depiction of a limitless and abundant universe with prosperity available to all. What's shifting is the whole notion that "prosperity" has to mean having a lot of money. In the new model of prosperity, we can all have as much as it takes to fulfill our highest purpose and live our greatest joy. For some of us this means having a lot of money and for others this requires much less. When we unhook the idea of prosperity from the prerequisite of having a lot of money, it becomes much easier to find our own personal path of thriving.

Exercise: What Do You Want?

If having more money is something you want, instead of focusing on the "more," consider the "what" and "why." If the truth of this universe is that you may have whatever will serve your highest good and happiness, what is it that you would like to create with more money?

I suggest putting this in writing as a way of clarifying your intent. Clearly identifying what you want will often call your intention into being more quickly and efficiently than will struggling to make enough money to afford the life you want.

If you don't have anything clearly in mind but just want more money, reflect on why. It may be that you are struggling to live up to old societal norms or striving for something that can't be purchased with more money. If we make money our goal without being clear about what we really want from it, we may succeed in creating more money but still not have the experiences of safety, self-worth, freedom, happiness, or love that are our true desires. It may even distract us from these deeper callings.

⬥⬥⬥⬥⬥⬥

True prosperity has nothing to do with money and how much of it we have. Prosperity is a state of mind and, when we have it, we automatically program our lives to work financially. Whether we have a lot or a little, we have our needs and wants fulfilled. We have the ability to attract more, without compromising our well-being in the process, and we are also able to create an abundant life without an abundance of money. If inwardly we feel lack, we'll never be satisfied with what we have. Consequently, no matter how much money we make, we'll create debt, struggle, and worry out of it.

One of my personal role models of prosperity is a remarkable woman who, in the 1950s, let go of her middle class life, took the name Peace Pilgrim, and spent the rest of her years, until she passed away in 1989, walking back and forth across the country talking to people about peace. She owned only one set of clothes and the very few personal items she could fit in her pockets. She ate only when she was offered food, slept indoors only when she was offered shelter, and experienced the world to be an overflowing banquet of God's abundance.

She felt freer the less she owned, and she lived a richly prosperous life filled with joy, purpose, good health and plenty of all she needed and wanted materially. By contrast, I've known many people who have extravagant incomes, beautiful homes, cars and other possessions but live in a state of chronic financial struggle. Many others have all the money they want but lack the time, health, or inner peace to enjoy their material abundance. Personally, I would rather have what Peace Pilgrim had.

Another one of my prosperity role models is Constance Kellough, the president of Namaste Publishing and the publisher of my first book, *Holding a Butterfly*. Constance got into the book publishing business when the then unknown author, Eckhart Tolle, asked if she would publish his book. Guided by her heart, she agreed, and since then has taken all kinds of so-called risks in the publishing business by listening to her heart and making world service her priority instead of following safe protocol and profits. By doing business this way, she became quite successful with a number of best-sellers, including Eckhart Tolle's *The Power of Now*.

My two role models couldn't be any more different on the outside, yet they share in common the attributes of extreme generosity, a desire to be of service, and a whole-hearted appreciation for the abundance of life.

Our last prosperity exercise here is aimed at cultivating the consciousness of prosperity that best supports your highest good. To do this we will again venture into the One Mind. So, before going into the next miracle experiment, think of someone who best demonstrates prosperity in the way you now want it to manifest in your life. This can be someone who you know personally or by reputation who, to the best of your knowledge, enjoys prosperity in the way you wish it for yourself.

Choose carefully. Pick a person who inspires you and with whom you feel a heart-felt resonance; not just the richest person you can name. Will it support your well-being to own an island and a jet or is it of greater importance to have a loving family, health, happiness, meaning and all the money you need for the home, vacations and material things that make life enjoyable? Who best embodies for you the happy life that you most want?

If you have difficulty identifying a specific individual, then make one up as though you are creating a character in a story. Be sure that the person you bring to mind has all of these characteristics:

- A high degree of generosity

- A strong sense of purpose and service

- A joyful spirit, including a joyful appreciation for the abundance of life

- Freedom from struggle and worry about money

- A lifestyle that reflects prosperity in the way you wish it for yourself

Miracle Experiment: Rising Together in Prosperity

Quiet your mind for a moment and let your attention float free. Take a deep breath or two to help you transition to a soft, open mental state...

Let your sense of identification shift from the density and limitation of matter to a bright, clear, beautiful energy that is your true essence. As you make this shift in perception you leave behind the limitations of dense matter and start to see the cells of your physical body lighting up and becoming radiant with this energy... And now, all the particles that make up your body are becoming lighter; the molecules, the atoms, the sub-atomic particles, all spreading out, vibrating in beautiful light.

See the bright energy of everyone in this miracle experiment network of souls, past, present and future, vibrating together now, in joined consciousness beyond the illusionary limits of space and time, each of us bringing only higher love to the whole. As a group we form a powerful network for healing and miracles.

Picture us all immersed in a beautiful, limitless sea of Universal Light. Call it as you wish: the Zero Point Field; the One Mind; God... Imagine it to be the essence of all beauty and wisdom; the source of absolute well-being; a sea of pure divine love.

Feel yourself held in the loving and blissful embrace of this limitless source, rocked in an ocean of light and breathing it in with every breath. You see that drawing deeply from this source doesn't mean there is less for anyone else, any more than your breathing deeply robs breath from others. This source is the pure absence of scarcity.

Imagine that you are not just held in this limitless field, you are a part of it; one with the light; one with the Source; one with God. Feel yourself as ever-flowing, abundant, never depleted no matter how much you outflow.

When you can imagine this, direct your attention to one person in our miracle experiment network of souls. You don't need to know who it is. Simply let their light draw you. You don't need to see a face or know a name, a place, or even a time. Now, as one with the limitless source, flow a current of abundant light and life energy to this person. This happens as easily as blowing a gentle breath their way.

The wave you send is Divine Source, so it will take whatever form the receiver most needs: healing, love, money, inspiration, opportunity, peace of mind. Flow your love and light to this soul with all the limitlessness and ease you now invite into your own life and know that the minute you're able to embody the abundance you want and give it whole-heartedly, you've already begun to attract the same to yourself.

Even though we may be separated in space and time, our minds and hearts joining in this work give it great power. That we've built the energy here repeatedly, through all the exercises we've done together outside of time, past, present, and future, gives it more power still. Having this significant energy with you right now creates an opening, if you're willing to reach for it, where a small intention can produce a life-changing result. So, as you continue to send a healing wave to another in our network, hold the intention that you are now creating a new pattern of energy flow in your life. How you send is how you will now receive, so feel the steadiness of the energy you're sending, the limitlessness of it, the ease, love, and joy of it. Know that whatever you can feel coming through you, will now start coming to you... Stay in this healing wave as long as you like, until it feels complete...

Take a break here or continue into the next part of this exercise:

Now that we've prepared ourselves on many levels to be truly ready for prosperity, it's time to meet your prosperity role model in the One Mind. In the One Mind we are joined in love with all beings, so even if your chosen mentor is not someone you know personally, know that the essence of this being loves you all the same.

Imagine this person is with you now, here to help you learn what they know about living a truly prosperous life. See your teacher look into your eyes with the deepest love. Just as you offered an unconditional gift of Divine Source to another, your role model now offers you that same gift.

Receive this sacred transmission so deeply that you feel your heart blending with your teacher's in pure Divine Love. And as this blending in love occurs, imagine that you are also absorbing this person's understanding and magnetism around prosperity. Imagine feeling the peace they feel around money and the ease they bring to its flow. Feel their zest for life and the joy they take in living purposefully. Most of all, feel with your role model the great pleasure of generosity; the miracle of being able to raise up another person with your gifts.

As you feel yourself completely resonant with this powerful vibration of your teacher's highest gifts, ripple it on to every soul in our miracle experiment network. Imagine that by joining with your teacher's vibration of prosperity and sharing it, you have made this person's unique wisdom available to us all.

Realize that many others have done the same, sharing a diverse range of wisdom around True Prosperity with you. Your spiritual bank account has been filled to overflowing with resources you haven't even imagined yet. Take a moment to let this in and feel the wonder of it!

Sit in gratitude for a moment and then return your attention to your body and your surroundings. Come back feeling refreshed and alert.

Exercise: See the World as your Role Model Does

From time to time over the next week or so, imagine yourself in the reality of your role model. Imagine seeing the world through their eyes and imagine all the ways they might feel and behave differently from you. Let yourself experience the inner peace they have around money and the attitudes they hold around its flow. Feel their zest for life, their joy in purpose, and their generous heart. Ask yourself what they might do in your circumstance.

Section III:

Evolution Revolution—

The Path of Spiritual Activism

One discovers the light in darkness. That is what darkness is for. But everything in our lives depends on how we bear the light. It is necessary, while in darkness, to know that there is a light somewhere, to know that in oneself, waiting to be found there is a light. What the light reveals is danger, and what it demands is faith...

James Baldwin

Chapter 14: Bringing the Towers Down

A great turning point in the first twenty-nine years of the Harmonic Convergence call to Unity came at the half-way mark, in September of 2001, the day that terrorists crashed planes into the World Trade Center in New York City. On that soul-shaking day of September 11, I sat in meditation with the powerful, even frightening, Tarot image of "The Tower." I dug this particular card out of my old, seldom-used Tarot deck that day because it depicts a lightning-struck tower collapsing, flames shooting out of its windows, people falling to the ground—an image chillingly the same as the one that was being shown repeatedly in the media that day and in the aftermath.

The whole of the Tarot portrays, through images, archetypal stages of growth and human experience. This image, the Tower, speaks of things that look strong and solid, yet are dead within and, as a result, are more vulnerable than they appear—as with a dead tree ready to fall with the next big storm.

Or like the powerful behemoth, the United States, sent into a downward spiral by a single terrorist attack. The Tower brings large, overblown structures tumbling to the ground so that something fresh and new can grow from the ground up. Though a necessary part of growth, it's seldom easy.

On that day, in shock, I sat with the Tarot image in front of me. The horror of a Tarot symbol coming to life in such a world-shaking way felt like a signal to me that we were all entering a challenging new era. I grieved and feared that day, not just for the horrific damage done but for all the painful crumbling of life as we knew it that I sensed coming. In retrospect, I've come to see this event in the context of an evolutionary call to Unity, but then I only saw an immediate future that looked bleak. It was only my faith in the deeper meaning of the archetype that gave me hope for the new beginning that inevitably must follow even the most painful ending.

The events of 9/11 had an almost a mythic quality. In the days following the attack, horrifying footage of the towers crashing down were played over and over and over, embedding them deeply inside us, not just as an event but as a landmark—both historic and deeply personal for those of us old enough to have lived through it.

Since then, much has crumbled as recounted earlier in this text: war, the economy, the environment... But perhaps even more significant than the many measurable costs is the bone-deep fear that has replaced Americans' previous sense of invulnerability. We've fallen from our ivory tower of illusion and lost the naïve belief that our money and force and stature will keep us safe. In a very profound way, we've all—America leading the way for much of the rest of the world—been collectively drawn into the archetypal myth and the spiritual work represented by the Tower.

As a symbol for our age, a towering skyscraper falling down is a fitting one. A skyscraper is so perfectly hierarchical and so seemingly inviolable; it houses us one on top of the other, disconnected from the earth, with the richest and most powerful at the very top. Its tumbling is dramatic and catastrophic, but, over time, amidst the rubble, tiny shoots grow, invisibly at first—our attention still eclipsed by the magnitude of the rubble. But after the passage of years, it becomes evident that where once stood a lifeless tower of people existing in isolation, there is now a field: alive, in bloom and filled with people interacting.

Metaphor, of course. Where the actual towers stood there is now a skyscraper even higher than before, but in the years following 9/11 there are a magnitude of "fields" that have grown up in the interactive era of the Web 2.0. One "field," in particular, is directly linked to 9/11 as Scott Heiferman, CEO and founder of Meetup, shared in a message he sent out to millions on September 10, 2011.[1]

In 2001, he lived just a couple of miles from Ground Zero. As a typical New Yorker, he didn't know or think about his neighbors, except to wish they weren't there, until the towers falling brought him out of his house and into a new exchange with his community: "You know, being neighborly," he wrote.

This unfamiliar interaction was so profoundly moving that he and a group of others wondered if the events of 9/11 could bring people together in a lasting way and thus the idea of Meetup was born—an internet structure to help people meet up around their interests and needs; a way to get people away from their computers to gather in person and form communities. There are now more than 100,000 Meetup groups with millions of members. In Heiferman's words, "Meetups aren't about 9/11, but they may not be happening if it weren't for 9/11."

The marker event of 9/11 was a collective experience that signaled the need for each of us individually to undertake the important work of releasing all that's become lifeless and limiting, the structures in our lives that may be familiar and easy, yet cut us off from the vital life force of the earth, other people, and our own spirit.

Perhaps a way to understand this collective abstraction in the context of personal experience is to consider the Tower as a symbol of everything that keeps us in a state of isolation: separate from our highest good, separate from our wisdom and power, separate from other people, from nature, from God. The Tower represents things that separate us from our conscience and from knowing our interrelatedness to all life as dramatically as a skyscraper separates us from the earth.

The image of the Tower in the Tarot is fraught with crisis and catastrophe, not because letting go has to be disastrous, but because when our human egos have to cope with the uncertainty of releasing what's familiar, we universally resist, not accepting change until the metaphorical tower crashes down with us still clinging to it.

Crisis and growth don't have to go hand in hand. Yet, what would spare us pain is often the hardest action to take—not the most painful, just the most abhorrent. Change without crisis requires a willing deconstruction of our "towers" at the first detection of weakness, before they crash down on us. It requires stepping out of complacency and comfort to work hard when we don't absolutely have to. It even means being willing to surrender that which has felt like our safest sanctuary. Most challenging of all, this work tends to bring us face to face with our own shadow, the dark and imperfect aspects of our self that we've defended against so well, we hardly see them at all.

But when we allow our personal armor to crack and we face ourselves honestly, we are suddenly free in a whole new way. Though this work is humbling, we are not bound to rigid conditioning and harsh expectations; we have choices. We can breathe and grow.

Exercise: Identifying and Bringing Down Your "Tower"

This exercise is another that works through the randomness of synchronicity, this time to give you a glimpse into the workings of your own shadow. The shadow is a part of us that's semi or completely unconscious. Synchronicity, set in motion through ritual and spiritual intent, is a helpful way to bypass the filters of ego and see things our conscious mind might miss or dismiss. Consequently, to receive the full benefit from this exercise, it's important to complete each step before reading ahead to the next.

Questions for Thought

- What change do you most want to bring into your life at this time?

- How have you been resisting change? Specifically, how have you been avoiding taking a next step that's been calling to you? How are you not letting go of what you no longer need? Are there ways in which you're choosing comfort over growth? How are you controlling too tightly out of fear instead of trusting the process of life?

The Ritual

In a room where you can have some private, undisturbed time, create five stations around the edges of the room, with a lit candle or other clear marker at each one. Identify them in some way as stations one, two, three, four, and five. For this meditation, darken the room if you can and create a comfortable seat for yourself in the middle.

Meditation

Relax your body and quiet your thoughts with some deep, slow breaths. Turn your attention inward and let your sense of identification shift from the small self of your personality and body to your spiritual Higher Self.

Imagine yourself as more than your body, thoughts, emotions, and personal history. Recognize yourself as a beautiful, radiant being of light and see the Higher Selves of the many others reading these words now joining you. We've all gathered, beyond the illusionary limits of space and time, in a magnificent, sacred arena in the spiritual realm. Together we form a powerful circle for spiritual awakening. In the spiritual realm time is an illusion, so you see the lights of all the souls in the miracle experiment network who have in the past and will in the future gather in this circle created by our intent.

Recognize how much stronger we are together than separately. It's not necessary that we ever meet face-to-face. Our joined intentions are enough to quicken our growth, awaken our intuition, and amplify our healing power. What has seemed difficult in the past will come more easily now. Take a moment to feel the energy of the circle building.

We've come together today to further the important work of bringing down the Towers of our world and to heal the painful illusions of separateness. We're not alone in this work; many souls are committed to it and our sincere desire to serve the highest good links us to forces of love much greater than our own personal power. Picture our circle of light linking to a much larger network of souls, creating an unstoppable force for good.

Yet, while we do this work with so many others, the next step is one we must take alone, because the Towers of separateness that plague our world have their roots within each of us.

So, imagine yourself gently relaxing into darkness now: this isn't the darkness we may equate with evil. This is the darkness of nighttime, of the unknown, of mystery and of unconsciousness. Imagine the dimming light making the darkness within yourself easier to see. Look deeply into the dark and see aspects of your personality that you've denied and hidden in the shadows.

First, take out and examine the part of yourself that clings to self-righteous anger and being right at the expense of being at peace; the side of you that would rather win than love and be loved. Simply be with this aspect of yourself. It's one that lives within each of us. Let go of judgment, shame and blame. Simply be present with yourself. Breathe... relax. Be present...

Next, look at your cheating, greedy side: the part that will grab a bit more for yourself at someone else's expense if you think you can get away with it. How have you taken something, even though it felt wrong? A little fudging on taxes? Failing to correct a mistake at the cash register? Cheating on a spouse? Leaving others to do your work? We all have a kernel of this cheater living within us. Don't judge, just be present with yourself...

Now, take a look at the fearful, controlling side of yourself. How are you overly critical of others? (If you believe you're only critical of yourself, look deeper.) How do you try to control and manipulate others to get your way? How do you try to control the events in your life? How do you even try to tell God what to do? Don't judge or try to explain, just be present...

Next, look at the miser that lives within you, the part that fearfully hoards what you have, be it material or emotional, and finds excuses not to share. Do you give materially, so you don't have to give love? Do you give time, so you don't have to share your money? Look at all that you withhold out of fear. Just breathe and be present with yourself...

Now see the side of yourself that prefers to do nothing at all. This is the part that doesn't take a stand for what's right; that looks the other way; that waits for someone else to do it and convinces yourself that you can't make a difference anyway, so why bother. How many important decisions have you made by making none at all? Relax into nonjudgment and be present...

Look at all the parts of yourself that are too shameful to bring out into the light of day: your lies and secrets, the things you don't want anyone to know about you, your hidden fears, petty acts, and shameful thoughts—all of it. Let the strength and support of so much loving consciousness around you help you to see more clearly than ever before all that you've kept hidden in the shadows of your own being.

For the moment, it's enough to simply face yourself. This in itself is a courageous act. Let go of judgment, shame, and blame and just be with yourself. Let go of explanations and justifications and just be. Let your body relax and your mind become still. Breathe. Be with yourself and be at peace.

Let all your walls of defense fall to pieces. Feel how much energy it takes to keep them in place; how exhausting it is to keep your secrets hidden. In this moment simply feel the relief of letting go of everything you feel you must manage and hold together. Relax and let go of being who you think you should be. Let go of control. Let go of blaming. Let go of guilt and shame. Breathe... relax... let go...

Now imagine one soul from our network of souls joining you, facing you, looking into your eyes. You don't know who it is; you just know that this particular soul has come to you in love. It could be someone from the past or future. It could be someone far away. It could be me. In this moment allow yourself to be seen. Reveal to this loving soul the fears you try not to show, the vulnerabilities you try to hide, the feelings of aloneness that come in the night, the things you try to control but can't quite, the dark angry parts and the things you can't forgive yourself for...

Imagine this other soul is seeing all of you, bearing witness to who you are, the best and worst of you, and is simply being present with you in love and acceptance. Our efforts to hide from one another don't really stop people from seeing us but they do keep us separate.

So, in the presence of this loving soul, let down your guard. Let yourself be seen, known, and accepted in your totality. Show the parts of yourself that are too imperfect or vulnerable to show, those things you've never shown anyone, the things you've hidden even from yourself. Stand completely vulnerable before this person. Imagine this soul is seeing you as God sees you: nothing hidden; nothing that can't be loved.

As you open to this loving connection, let go of everything you think you are: being good, being bad, being right, being afraid, being angry, being not good enough, being special, being a victim, being in control. Let them all fall away. Let go of knowing who you are for certain. Just let go and be.

With all that you've released, who are you now free to be? What's possible that wasn't before? Open your mind to the higher plan Spirit may have for you when you let go and make space...

Thank this helper soul and let your attention come gently back to the room around you. Preserving your meditative state, gently rise and slowly walk around the room, taking in the five stations. Taking as much time as you need, allow yourself to be drawn to one of them. Whatever station you pick will have an important message for you. Know that you can't pick the wrong one, so there's no need to think as you do this. Simply walk peacefully, being in the surrendered place of your meditation until you're ready to choose a station. When you've found your place, read on.

ϕϕϕϕϕϕϕϕ

Some of the Towers Common to Us All

For anyone ready to undertake the courageous work of bringing your own inner Tower down before it collapses, the following is an articulation of some of the more powerful Towers that drive our world, and the seductive messages they scream in our heads. Each one is followed by the quieter whisper of Spirit that always offers another option precisely where we're sure none exist.

As you read through these, notice which Towers have the strongest hold on you and ask yourself what it would take for you to bring this construction down willingly without it taking a life crisis to motivate you to action.

- **The Tower of Judgment and Blame** offers a seamless debate. It says, "My way is the right way! I know I'm right, why should I be the one to back down? Forgiveness needs to be earned. It's their fault. I'm justified in putting those who've hurt me out of my heart."

    (What would I do differently if I loved peace as much as I have loved being right? If world peace depended upon my forgiveness, would I be willing?)

- **The Tower of Complacency,** the great procrastinator, lulls us to sleep: "It's easier not to. I can do it later. I'm comfortable where I am. If I look the other way I won't have to get involved."

    (What would I do differently if I valued joy and fulfillment even more than I value comfort?)

- **The Tower of No Faith** buries us in self-pity: "Good things happen to other people, not me. God is far away/doesn't exist/doesn't listen. It's too late/too hard/too impossible. One person can't really make a difference."

    (What would I do differently if I believed, beyond a shadow of a doubt, that everything I do and think makes a difference?)

- **The Control Tower** disguises fear and self-loathing behind a mask of perfectionism and tells us, "If I control everything, I'll be safe. No one can do it as well as me. I don't trust people/God to be there when I need them. If I can't know and control all the details of my next step, I'm not moving."

  (If I just let everything fall to pieces and found that I had survived, that the world had survived without me, who would I be then, and what would I be free to do?)

- **The Fear-Ridden Greed Tower** warns us of imminent scarcity: "There's not enough of anything good to go around so I need to hold on to what I have and amass more. I need to think of myself first because nobody else will."

  (If I understood that I only get to keep what I'm willing to lovingly share, what would I do with the material and intangible riches I have held the tightest?)

Your Tower

Each of the stations you made in your room corresponds to one of these five Towers. If you didn't read ahead in the exercise, your conscious mind didn't know which station represents which Tower, but your intuitive mind did, and you've been guided to the one that most stands in the way of your highest good at this time. If you chose station 1, the Tower of "Judgment and Blame" is the one that most need's your attention. If you chose station 2, it's the Tower of Complacency. Station 3 is the Tower of No Faith. Station 4 is the Control Tower. Station 5 is the Tower of Greed.

Action

Review what's written about this Tower and honesty reflect on how this expression of separateness is currently driving your life. Feel our circle of light and the greater network of souls still present with you, amplifying your insight, courage, and power to change. Read the healing option of Spirit that corresponds to your Tower and find as many ways to act in this manner as you can over the next week.

Closing the Ritual

Complete your ritual by thanking the souls in our circle, the greater network of souls, and all the invisible forces of Love and Light that have been with us. If you'd like, make an affirmative declaration related to healing your Tower of separateness. For example: "All that I have I share in love because I know love comes back to me multiplied." Or, "I now choose love over blame." Or, "I now trust God, myself, and the process of life." When your experience feels complete, blow out your candles.

More Questions for Thought

- What physical structures of your life that once seemed solid have fallen apart in your most recent history? This would include unexpected changes in circumstance that resulted in loss, such as losing a job, losing a relationship, loss of health, death of a loved one, or any kind of disruptive change in the solid predictability of your life.

- Assume that whatever fell apart created a sacred space for something important to enter. What do you imagine this to be?

Chapter 15: Healing the Collective Shadow of our Times

Just ten days after the 2016 presidential election of Donald Trump, the Southern Poverty Law Center reported a huge spike in the number of hate incidents—some 400 reported in one week, many of them among school children[1]. In the following month, this number continued to rise dramatically, often with assaulters shouting Trump's name.

The Ku Klux Klan and the American Nazi Party, who both enthusiastically endorsed Trump, praised his cabinet appointments. These hate groups, that once were widely considered unacceptable fringe organizations, celebrated a new time in the sun with new credibility following the election. Donald Trump's win wasn't simply the Republican winning over the Democrat.

Regardless of party, presidential frontrunners have historically gone to great lengths to portray "presidential" qualities of dignity, restraint and grace befitting a head of state. One misstep can ruin a career in the way Howard Dean's notorious primal scream ended his presidential run in 2004. None of this was the case with Donald Trump, whose demeanor much more resembled that of the adolescent play yard bully, pushing every limit to see how much could be gotten away with. Even noxious recordings of him bragging about sexual assault didn't keep him from winning an election.

What happened with the Trump election was more than a simple Republican/Democrat divide—Republicans and Democrats alike looked on in horror as a new United States government increasingly resembled a White Nationalist hate group. This trend was sweeping other parts of the world as well, with neo-Nazi activity and nationalist sentiments on the rise all throughout Europe, the British "Brexit" being just one manifestation of growing dislike for immigrant and non-mainstream populations.

By early 2017, it was clear that Donald Trump was a president like no other. With polls showing him to be the most unpopular president ever, he was also the most famous—perhaps infamous—man in the world. In a New York Times article, Farhad Manjoo wrote that he tried to spend an entire week avoiding Trump-related news but, finding it incredibly difficult, concluded that, "Coverage of Mr. Trump may eclipse that of any single human being ever."[2]

For better or worse, when something or someone is hammered into our consciousness in such an all-day, every-day way, it becomes part of our collective unconscious; it begins to symbolize something for all of us and becomes part of our collective mythology. The twenty-nine-year evolutionary journey that began with the seeding of a Unity impulse at the Harmonic Convergence has had a shadow side throughout. At the half-way point of this journey, about fourteen years later, when Saturn opposed its position in 1987—a stressful time in the life of any entity—this shadow side burst vividly into our collective awareness with the fall of the Towers on 9/11. With an ironic and seemingly deliberate play on symbols, the full-circle Saturn return point of the journey in 2016 brought us the image of the overblown, almost caricature-ish Trump Tower.

At this significant coming of age point of the Harmonic Convergence and of humanity's evolution, what we saw emerging in the form of this unconventional U.S. president was the reflection of our collective shadow now completely exposed. Carl Jung, father of transpersonal psychology, used the term "shadow" to refer to a part of the unconscious personality consisting of personal, unknown aspects of the ego that we are more likely to see in others (and feel an emotional charge around) than recognize in ourselves. In Jung's last book, *Man and His Symbols*, a collection of writings by his closest colleagues that he edited, Dr. Marie-Louise von Franz writes of this process:

> "If people observe their own unconscious tendencies in other people, this is called a 'projection.' Political agitation in all countries is full of such projections, just as much as the backyard gossip of little groups and individuals. Projections of all kinds obscure our view of our fellow men, spoiling its objectivity, and thus spoiling all possibility of genuine human relationships.
>
> And there is an additional disadvantage in projecting our shadow. If we identify our own shadow with, say, the communists or the capitalists, a part of our own personality remains on the opposing side. The result is that we shall constantly (though involuntarily) do things behind our own backs that support this other side, and thus we shall unwittingly help our enemy."[3]

In this pivotal era of breakdown or breakthrough, I believe we chose Donald Trump to be the Leader of the Free World because collectively there are now enough of us who are ready to do the most difficult work of healing the Shadow. Our collective shadow of hatred and separateness is no longer covered up by anything. The collective conversation of White America that used to say, at least on the surface, that we as a nation do not ascribe to racism, misogyny and xenophobia, is now saying, "The president does it, so I can too." In fact, this is exactly what a little boy said to a little girl in the week after the election when he grabbed her crotch and sent her home from school traumatized[4].

Having all this out in the open isn't an altogether bad thing. What we won't see, we can't change. Fifteen years earlier, on 9/11 when the towers came down, we became viscerally aware of the dangerous "Other." Back then, the Other was in a foreign land and we went to war to fight them there so they wouldn't come here. We kept our collective shadow at a safe distance, even though no amount of fighting seemed to be enough to keep us "safe." But by 2016, the Other had become us. The whole presidential campaign gave us permission to openly hate. And then, suddenly, the Other was no longer Isis in our midst, it was the kid next door ripping hijabs off the heads of young girls. It was our neighbor painting "Trump Nation, Whites Only" on the church down the street and swastikas showing up in the park. It was our uncle who used the "N" word in our presence for the first time.

With the election of Trump, the status of the U.S. president as "Leader of the Free World" became questionable but perhaps this POTUS was leading the world in the painful work of revealing the shadow. Coming face to face with one's own shadow is a shocking thing—it's so much more comfortable to see it from a distance in the reflection of someone else. Perhaps this is why so many Americans experienced a wave of shock following the 2016 election that felt deeply personal and wounding in a way no other election had. On some level, we're seeing ourselves and we're horrified.

If we're ever to heal this collective shadow of White America, a nation that was founded upon genocide and slavery, we can no longer blame anyone outside of ourselves for the dirty work of the Other. The Other hasn't just moved in next door, it's within each of us. As Elizabeth Kubler Ross frequently said, "We each have an inner Hitler and an inner Mother Theresa." The opportunity here is to learn compassion—and not just for the victims of bullies but for the victimizers as well.

Our times have everything to do with recognizing who we have been, who we are in the darkest corners of our own hearts, and who we will choose to become. There are many opportunities before us—such as the opportunity to actively participate in our society instead of allowing 20% of the electorate to bring the worst of us into power. Nearly half of eligible voters did not participate in the 2016 election and significantly less that this in mid-term elections. Many, many people who did not want Donald Trump as president chose him all the same through non-action.

There's also a choice here to learn compassion. Not sympathy or pity, but the willingness to understand the Other deeply enough that we can no longer maintain the illusion of being separate. This election didn't just bring out underlying racism, sexism and xenophobia, it turned friends and family against one another because they fell on different sides of the voting divide.

Here is the simplest of healing exercises to start this process.

Exercise: Healing

Take a moment to picture in your mind's eye whoever represents the Other to you: the one who feels wrong, foreign, perhaps even shocking in their wrong-mindedness. It may be a politician; it may be your neighbor or Facebook friend; it may be a family member who holds different values to you.

If you have judgments or outrage, you don't need to resolve these now. Simply put these feelings to the side so that in this moment you can see this individual through the eyes of Higher Spiritual Truth that recognizes how connected we all are. See this individual as a being worthy of love, as is every living being. Recognize the higher truth that withholding love from this being only harms you, and because we are all One, what harms you harms everyone.

Imagine how it feels to be this person.

What do you imagine their fears are? What do you imagine wakes them up in the middle of the night? Can you imagine the ways in which this person has felt unloved, inadequate or undeserving? What do you imagine they are inwardly crying out for? Let you heart break open in compassion for this person's pain and fear.

Now, from your heart, send the simplest of prayers: "I love and bless you." Even if your personality doesn't quite feel it, ask your Higher Self to transmit this prayer with sincerity. Love is the new paradigm of our times. It puts everything to right. It's the only way to take the wind out the sails of bullies whether we find them at the highest level of governing, or on the playground, or within our own hearts. "I love and bless you..." Say it to our politicians; say it to your neighbors; say it to the dark, shameful thoughts in your own mind. Just as we all have an inner saint, we also all have an inner bully. With love, only the highest can happen.

I love and bless you.

Chapter 16: Rising Above Fear

September 11, 2001, when the Twin Towers fell, marked the beginning of a new era of collective, escalating fear. If environmental uncertainties, financial stresses and rising global terrorism weren't enough, by 2016 Trump-induced anxiety became a real disorder with therapists around the country noticing an extreme uptick in their client loads as a result. With 75% of the electorate not voting for Trump, as well as a large citizen and non-citizen immigrant population feeling particularly targeted, the United States became a nation in shock, anxiety and even terror.

A much-tweeted quote by Deepak Chopra suggests that, "All fear is ultimately the fear of mortality in disguise—the fear of change." Many of us live in constant fear of dying without even realizing that it's death we fear. We might call it loss, change, endings, or feeling out of control. Even if we rarely give the subject of death a thought, the reality of this absolute ending and ultimate loss of control is always with us, affecting how we go about life.

In my home town of Minneapolis, in August of 2007, a highly trafficked bridge collapsed in the middle of town at rush hour. A wave of shock rippled, not just through the Twin Cities, but through the nation, as the story hung in the national news for many days. The shock seemed larger than the tragedy of the thirteen people killed. After all, we hear of much greater numbers killed all the time. Just weeks after the bridge incident, fourteen soldiers were killed in Iraq and, by the next day, it was already old news. But the bridge was different. It was that something we took for granted, something we never thought to fear—the highway we all drove upon every day—could kill us. We all know the world's a dangerous place and that terrible things happen. It's when they happen in ways we least expect that we feel shaken.

This is what makes acts of terrorism so successful—they take us by surprise. And this is when we become willing to spend billions and trillions on everything from airport security to foreign wars, all in the name of protecting ourselves, not so much from actual danger but from feeling so frighteningly out of control. We spend resources on what security expert Bruce Schneier calls "the theater of security" instead of on what could more effectively save us—like new bridges. But when bad things happen unexpectedly it's an all too human response to focus on doing whatever we can to keep it from ever happening again.

We rarely stop to wonder at these times why some come through unscathed. When the Minneapolis bridge fell into the Mississippi, there were many stories of miraculous survivals: one woman was knocked unconscious by the collapse, woke up in her car *under water,* and escaped to tell the story; a bus full of children were all rescued safely in spite of being just feet from an exploding truck. Think about it... this was a major highway at rush hour; it was thick with rush hour traffic; there was even a construction crew at work, but only thirteen died. That's a miracle.

One who has asked the question, "Why do some survive?" is Carolyn Miller in her fascinating book, *Creating Miracles,*[1] where she interviewed many people who'd experienced miraculous escapes from what would ordinarily be certain death or dire harm situations. Whether the situation was of driving off a cliff, maneuvering an out-of-control vehicle through speeding traffic, or dealing with deadly attackers, many people shared a common experience just as death or attack looked inevitable. As they recognized the very worst was about to happen, instead of a fight, flight or freeze response, they became very peaceful and calm. Fear diminished, and their perspective broadened to include a concern for the others present. Those in the midst of vehicle crashes spontaneously acted to save their passengers or those in an oncoming vehicle. Those being attacked were able to step out of the victim role and show compassion and kindness to their abusers. When their perspective shifted, a miracle happened. The attacker peacefully left or the maneuver aimed at sparing the lives of other motorists turned out to save the driver as well. This state is reminiscent of Larry Dossey's description of One Mind states where people heroically act to save another because their consciousness so spontaneously blends with the person in need that their fear for themselves vanishes.

These examples suggest that "safety" and "protection" aren't the same thing at all. Protection is a defense against all that we fear. It's often costly and depleting, and it offers no guarantee that we will be safe. As we've seen in the effort to combat terrorism since 9/11, sometimes all our efforts toward defense backfire and create more of what we fear the most. *A Course in Miracles* teaches that safety lies in our defenselessness. Perhaps the only thing that can truly keep us safe is a state of mind, as those who've tapped the One Mind have found. Instead of depleting our every last ounce of energy, be it through personal anxiety or the spending of national resources, to protect ourselves against all conceivable danger (and still winding up vulnerable to the inconceivable), we could do something to create safety.

As the once-traditional American mind set of "Give me liberty or give me death" increasingly devolves into "Take my civil liberties! Just don't let a terrorist get me!", maybe it's time to rethink our whole relationship with fear. Simply put, the more fear drives us, the more we'll inevitably find things to fear, and the more it will consume us. Perhaps we need to consider that there may be worse things than death, such as a life lived in fear. The wearisome toil of living in survival mode, protecting ourselves from all things frightening is never-ending, ever-escalating and it ultimately obliterates our capacity to fully live.

Yet, we live in a world that is increasingly manifesting the very dangers that come from our massively shared delusion of fear and there is no doubt that our collective stress level is escalating. The American Psychological Association, that has been tracking Americans' stress every year since 2007, reported an upswing in 2017 with more than half of Americans citing the political climate as being a significant source of stress, two-thirds saying the same about the future of our nation, and an increase in the number of people citing concern for their physical safety as being a significant source of stress.[2] Fear is in the air and if we don't address it in a head-on, intentional way, we're likely to breathe it in as unconsciously as we take in oxygen. In the same way that crisis is igniting our evolution in so many ways, escalating fear may be just the push that helps us break through to safety—true safety that can only be found in a state of consciousness.

From an entirely different perspective, some psychics and metaphysicians also speak of these times as being extraordinarily stressful but not because of terrorists and politics. One such spiritual teacher is Linda Dillon, a well-known psychic medium and author. Dillon, who connected with the One Mind following a near-death experience in 1984, now claims to receive messages from a council of higher beings. She says that we are experiencing a "tsunami of love" to the planet. In a June 2016 channeling session she said, "The energies that are penetrating the planet in this very moment are stronger than have ever been felt. For many it is creating a bit of a roller-coaster ride..."[3]

Looking for the best way to support my students in these times of change, I consulted one of the faculty members of my online Miracles Course program, Reverend Deb Teramani, a psychic medium who has been able to see and communicate with angels and nonphysical beings since childhood. She holds much the same view as Linda Dillon, that we are collectively in the midst of an extraordinary process of ascension. In our conversation, Rev. Deb and I discovered that we both had been feeling intuitively guided in a similar direction—toward inner child work— and we both felt the same initial resistance to it.

Inner child work—really? Been there, done that, it's so 1980s! 1987 to be exact, with the release of *Healing the Child Within* by Charles Whitfield, M.D. and then a few years later the release of *Homecoming: Reclaiming and Championing Your Inner Child* by John Bradshaw. By the nineties, inner child work had become a movement.

But in a world that sometimes leaves us wanting to pull the covers over our heads and not leave our beds, perhaps calming the frightened child within is precisely what's needed. And, as with so many things that began in 1987 and are now coming of age, it's time to approach this work in a whole new context of importance: with an understanding that the healing work that was planted in our collective psyche back then, along with the vibration of Unity consciousness, is ready to be more fully assimilated now.

Another aspect of my conversation with Rev. Deb related to the importance of a literal shift in perspective—I now think of it as a One Mind perspective—that enables an experience of the world beyond fear. Rev. Deb described this state to me and, soon after, I had an extremely vivid experience of it in meditation. It involves "seeing" from a visual perspective slightly above and behind the back of the head. This is a shift out of the familiar sense of "self" that we tend to locate behind our physical eyes.

The experience of seeing from this perspective left me feeling very at peace, and very aware of the illusionary nature of physical reality. In this state, there was no place to go, nothing missing, nothing to fear, nothing to want or heal. I felt completely safe and unafraid of any change that could come my way. Essentially, it was a state of transcending the cyclical wheel of experience that lifts us into exhilaration one moment and tumbles us into suffering the next. This state is totally free of attachment. It doesn't discern anything as good or bad. Everything just is, and everything is connected. There is no path or outcome because everything is here now. So there are no agendas, goals, or aspirations. There's no need to manifest, heal, or change anything because there's such a clear awareness of the illusionary nature of the physical realm.

This state is the antithesis of the extreme experiences of our times that include "tsunamis of love" and people coming together as never before, as well as unprecedented corruption and frightening events happening almost daily. The physical world around us has never seemed more real and we are called as never before to live in a paradox: to step up with unconditional commitment to change the physical world for the better, and to step back from our attachment to any of it.

The exercise here will first address the human side of us that is still held back by childhood wounds and old patterns, and then will focus on awakening the higher consciousness that is simply beyond all that. Both phases of this work are important: the latter facilitates spiritual transcendence and the first phase deepens all-important spiritual maturity which empowers us to use transcendent experiences to thrive.

Exercise: Beyond Fear

Quiet your mind for a moment and let your attention float free. Take a deep breath or two to help you transition to a soft, open mental state...

Allow to come into your awareness the child part of you that somewhere along the way felt abandoned, disappointed, unloved and unsafe. You may have specific memories come to mind of needing something that wasn't there for you. Just let all this come to mind...

This child from long ago is still present inside of you and still feels empty, unloved, afraid, or not good enough... Just relax in the presence of this old hurt and, as the adult you are now, picture, and be with, the child you were then. See what age the child is. Notice what the child is wearing and where you imagine the child to be. What is the emotional state of the child: silent, or crying, or angry or scared? How does the child show what's going on inside? What or whom does the child need that isn't there? How is this experience shaping and changing this child? Let yourself grieve for this young person who deserves better. Let yourself feel sad or angry over what might have been for this child if they had been cared for differently...

Be aware though, that now the only one who can save this child and give what's needed is you. So in this moment, reach out to this child and give the love, the protection, the reassurance, the affirmation, the support, and whatever else was absent then. Comfort this child as a loving parent would reach out to their child in pain... Love this young person as the most precious child of God... See the child's affect begin to change: first from pain into trust... then into confidence... and soon into playfulness... and now joy.

Take them into your heart now because the adult you've become needs this child in order to thrive. This isn't the screaming child that runs your life into a ditch. This one is the keeper of your innocence and vitality; your spontaneity and creativity; your joy and passion for life; your ability to have faith and trust the process of life. So let the adult and the child become one, no longer separate and estranged.

The estrangement between you and this child has formed the core issues of your life that have resulted in recurring limitations and pain. If you have worked on these patterns in the past and they continue to surface, recognize that these times are like no other and you have resources available that you never had before.

For the first time now, look around and see that you are not alone, and have never been. See many beings of light surrounding you, always with you, loving you and celebrating every step of your journey, absolutely free of judgment. See the field of energy created by all of us in the miracle experiment network holding you in a web of light that keeps you safe and lifts you into realms of thriving that were never available to you before.

And now go a little deeper in your reflection...

Imagine that the dense matter of your physical body is becoming less heavy. You can start to see the cells of your physical body lit up and radiant with this energy... All the particles that make up your body are becoming less dense: the molecules, the atoms, the sub-atomic particles spreading out, vibrating in beautiful light. You look at your hands and see that the physical matter of your hands and arms is becoming transparent, no longer solidly opaque. In fact, the outline of your entire body is becoming something shadowy and vague.

Your focus now becomes broad—on everything and on nothing. There's a dissolving and melting taking place. It's not one you can see, define, or completely comprehend but you know it's in divine order. Parts of you relax that you didn't even know were tense. You set down burdens you didn't realize you were carrying. You can feel a layer of defensive armoring in your body that you never knew was there before, now melting away... Solid forms that you've been holding in place turn to smoke, releasing you from illusionary obligations... Things that were frozen now become fluid... Everything you thought you knew is now fuzzy. What was sharp has become soft...

The past and the future melt into a continuous NOW, and now there is nowhere to be, nothing to do, nothing that's knowable... so you surrender to the softness around you. Internal pressure gives way to peace...

The boundaries of your "self" soften and blur and there is no inside and outside; no here and there; no object and space; as all "things" blur together into continuity... In this softening, there is no "you." There just "is." This blending, merging, and flowing into Oneness isn't frightening or confusing. There is peace... deep peace... and peace gently gives way to something greater, something ecstatic... something that has no words... Relax into wordlessness, into Oneness, and just be...

Gently now, out of this ocean of oneness, you become aware of your own inner light—your light that is One with ALL THAT IS, yet still uniquely your own. Within this light, all your needs are met. There is perfect peace and deep contentment with what is. Within this light is all the happiness you have ever wanted. There is no desire to aspire to anything because everything is here. There is nothing to want because nothing is missing. There is nothing to fear because we have always been whole and complete and nothing can change that. There is nothing to resist or distrust. There is no past or future. There just... is. And all is well.

You can see all of us in the miracle experiment network together, everyone's light shining brightly, and with each, you can see a vague outline of the human body through which they express their light in the physical realm. But these physical outlines are pale and shadowy—not real. Mainly you see their lights. With no solid boundaries separating us, we merge in light. Even as we merge, each person's light is perfectly unique and wondrous, and it's a delight to touch and blend, light to light.

Picture other people in your life and see them as bright lights shining through the shadowy, not-real outline of their physical form. You become aware of how inadequately our human selves interact, sometimes clashing, sometimes disconnecting, lost in the illusion of separateness and not able to see the truth of our Oneness. But now, no matter what the human relationship is between you, know that the only true thing connecting you is love and light.

Picture the shadowy reality of your physical forms going through all the motions of day-to-day life together, rising and falling in elation, disappointment, fear, or anger as illusionary dramas play out. All the while, the light beings that we are remain connected in peaceful unity, no need for hope or fear... just the knowledge of love.

Imagine walking around in your world this way... your physical body a mere shadow, the inner light the only part of you that's real and true. Imagine that you're seeing the world around you from a location a little above your physical head. All the material world realities seem so inconsequential now; a mere playground for us to learn, deepen and evolve through the challenges and joys of physical existence.

As you experience reality from this elevated perspective, shift back for a moment. Let your awareness drop back down into your body's perspective and notice how real the physical world becomes; how Oneness becomes separateness; how the light dims and fear is more present. Notice how consuming this reality is and how easy it is to be lost in it...

Now go back up; your body becoming shadowy and transparent again; the light is all that's real, deep peace and wholeness are the true reality.

Now invite this awareness of spiritual reality to become an ongoing part of your perception. Ask to have this portal into higher consciousness awakened so that, as you go about your life, you find peace in the midst of change; so that you see the big picture beyond the ups and downs of life; so that you become a stabilizing and harmonizing influence on the world around you; and so that you easily thrive even as many around you struggle.

Imagine a beautiful light flowing in through the top of your head and down the length of your body... and a light flowing up from the earth into your feet and out the top of your head...

As you're ready, come back gently. Feel the boundaries of your body intact yet open to allow something new. Feel that your mind has been cleared and your body rejuvenated. You now have peace where before there was pressure.

Take some deep breaths, stretch, take your time... Come back to a normal waking state feeling refreshed, alert, grounded and awake.

Chapter 17: All Together Now—Breaking Through

In times of rapid change, old patterns tend to surface with a vengeance, making it feel as though things are falling apart and moving backward as quickly as forward. Painful though this may be, it's how we see clearly what has become dysfunctional and needs to be changed. Look, for example, at the resurgence of racial tensions in the United States since we collectively took the historic step of electing the first African American president (which also happened very close in time to the significant 2008 stress point related to the Harmonic Convergence). It's not that a black president made us more racist; it just brought it out into the open and has forced a new level of scrutiny. It has also been the catalyst for a growing Black Lives Matter movement, bringing heightened solidarity to marginalized communities as well as greater light and consciousness to what needs to change.

An historic example of backward movement spurring a leap forward happened at the same time as the 2008 presidential election. California voters approved a ban on same-sex marriage—the now-notorious "Prop 8"—taking away marriage rights that had been granted only six months earlier. This reversal of progress mobilized the gay and gay-allied community in a way it hadn't been since the height of the AIDS epidemic in the 1980s. This high level of activism propelled nation-wide marriage rights forward faster than anyone expected.

2016 saw much attention given to women's rights. The light and dark of these issues were starkly contrasted as Hillary Clinton came close to becoming the first woman president of the United States while the ugliness of sexual assault against women was prominent in the news, with such high-profile offenders as actor Bill Cosby, Fox News founder Roger Ailes, and Donald Trump. Many of these offenses were decades old due to the female victims being intimidated into silence by the powerful status of their abusers. But by 2016 women had become emboldened to speak out.

The subsequent election of Donald Trump might seem like an enormous step backward for women's rights but just days after he took office, the largest and most peaceful worldwide demonstration in history took place: Women's March of January 21, 2017. I was present myself at one of these gatherings that totaled an estimated 100,000 people, and was struck by the atmosphere of "Love Trumping Hate." The sense that we had come out *for* one another seemed greater than anything we had come out against. Contrasted with the highly angry and often violent demonstrations of the so called "peace and love" generation nearly fifty years earlier, I believe Women's March hinted at a new possibility emerging for activism that is based more in unity than outrage, where unprecedented numbers of people can be together—even in protest—in an atmosphere of loving solidarity where there is no violence and the change agent is love.

To put this in spiritual terms, I see this as a collective resurgence of the Divine Feminine. The archetype of the Divine Feminine embodies such qualities as community, connection, stewardship of resources and egalitarian forms of power. This influence has been sadly lacking in Western Civilization for centuries where patriarchal influences have prevailed, including the dominance of man over the earth, the dominance of men over women, and hierarchical power structures that enable some to hold dominance over others. In these highly transitional times, we may well see continued waves of backlash to each new wave of peace, yet the presence of peace is significant and, moving forward, I believe we will see that the evolution revolution will have women clearly leading the way.

While the Trump election was shocking to many, the immediate result was an unprecedented call to Unity. The era of egalitarian movements that grew out of the development of the internet in the 21st century, now escalated into a quantum leap forward. One such movement bears the name of the times: "Indivisible." This is the title of a twenty-six-page guide written by former congressional staffers that was released even before the Trump inauguration, and teaches groups how to locally resist the Trump agenda. As stated in the guide it is a *"resistance built on the values of inclusion, tolerance, and fairness."* The guide went viral, seeding thousands of local groups in just a matter of weeks.

As hate crimes rose in 2015-16 spurred by the Trump presidential run, in 2017, masses turned out to support targeted communities. Many showed up at airports around the country to protest Donald Trump's travel ban on seven primarily Muslim countries—again these protests had a strong feeling of being *for* one another as much as they were about protesting an issue.

A notable example of the shift from hate to love was the Texas Muslim Capital Day, a gathering of Muslims to encourage political participation. At the 2015 gathering, protesters were highly disruptive, shouting, "Mohammed is dead!" One woman succeeded in grabbing the microphone away from the speaker to loudly, "stand against the false prophet of Mohammed." The next Texas Muslim Capital Day took place in early February of 2017. This time, only one protester was there but, even more significantly, over two thousand non-Muslim volunteers showed up to create a human chain around the gathering and keep it safe from disruption. According to organizers of the effort, more than four times more people showed up than they had expected.[1]

This is all to say that if you have any personal sense of the forward momentum of your life reversing, or that issues you've been working on for years are still plaguing you, consider that it may have more to do with some part of you surging forward and causing the last remnant of old patterns to surface with a vengeance so they can be released. As a great evolutionary shift from separateness to Unity pulls and pushes at us, we receive glimpses of a higher reality empowered by love, then whatever old patterns aren't in alignment with this new energy start kicking and screaming, drawing us back into the more familiar consciousness of limitation, separateness and fear. As much as we might despise the limitations we've fought against, there's comfort in the familiar even as there's pain, and we often seek it without even realizing we're doing so. This is when life seems to fall apart and we have a sense of backward progress. However, it's this very sense of "moving backward" that mobilizes the next surge of consciousness and growth—growth that comes not in the old way, from the top down or through pulling ourselves up by our bootstraps, but from the ground up, collectively through wide scale activism and through tapping the power of all of us together.

If there are personal challenges that you have struggled with for a long time but haven't been able to transform or transcend, perhaps it's because you haven't been approaching them in the new way of community and collective resources. What has seemed impossibly out of reach in the past can come far more easily now if we are willing to step beyond our ingrained habits of self-sufficiency.

For example, I sometimes give participants in my workshops a simple instruction to create this moment to be as full and rich as they would like the rest of their lives to become. I give no other instructions about how to do this. I even sit out of the resulting experience so people will know that whatever they create is their doing and not mine.

Typically, groups go through a period of haggling about what to do. Egos flare and personalities clash. Frequently, individuals start to break off from the group to do their own thing in the corners of the room with a feeling that they can't get their needs met any other way. Sometimes this exercise will result in an amazing array of competing pandemonium. In one corner, several might be grouped around a piano having a singalong. Somewhere else, two others are having a quiet, serious conversation, while still others are dancing and playing games, trying desperately to create "fun." Then there is the occasional, lost-looking individual, sitting alone, looking frightened as he or she is completely ignored by everyone else.

After these experiences, where all but a few look like they're having a wonderful time, I ask everyone to share how they were feeling. In spite of working so hard to have a good time, it's rare that anyone enjoys these chaotic sessions. Many wind up feeling angry, fearful and alienated. Some feel ashamed at how completely they had ignored someone alone and scared in the corner. For many, the exercise brings into sharp relief patterns of behavior that have long kept their lives from moving forward; behaviors meant to be self-preserving but that inevitably left them feeling unhappy. Many ingrained assumptions about life surface in this exercise—in particular, the fear that everyone in a group can't get what they need, especially not together and at the same time. In practice, however, as everyone separately strives to make their own little piece of the whole perfect for themselves, everyone fails, ending up disappointed and angry.

Sometimes, though, a group will make a shift from this Darwinian, survival of the fittest mode of operating, and leap to a higher level of functioning. It might start as one person reaches out to someone sitting alone and in pain. Suddenly two people are speaking to each other from their hearts, dropping social facades. One by one, others in the group are drawn in by the authenticity of this interaction, and soon the separate, chaotic groupings spontaneously come together to support the healing of one person.

By the end of this type of experience, people have instinctively moved closer to one another. Everyone is engaged. You can see it in body language as everyone leans in. There is a feeling of love and trust shared by all. When asked how they feel after such a session, all participants invariably report feeling very good and fulfilled. After an experience like this, even with less visible displays of laughing and celebrating, and even though only one person is the actual focus of attention, participants report feeling successful at the exercise of creating the moment to be as rich and full as they want their futures to become.

The breakthrough for all comes as a whole group spontaneously shifts into compassion for a single individual. Compassion, even when it comes with tears and the acknowledgment of pain, proves to be a more satisfying state than all the singing, dancing and "fun" that came before. It shifts everyone into a higher vibrational state and into a bonded, unified consciousness where one person's transformation is strongly felt by everyone. The whole group becomes able to osmose a bit of the healing and growth experienced by the single individual who was the focus. In this bonded state of group consciousness, one individual takes everyone where they most need to go. And this is just the point of our next exercise as we open to having a breakthrough.

Questions for Thought

Reflect for a moment on any ways that you may be feeling the push and pull of the evolutionary shift from separateness to Unity in your own life.

- What stresses of life seem to be intensifying?

- What is falling apart so that something new can be born?

- What repeating, painful patterns in your life seem to be resurfacing?

- How in your life are you feeling a sense of urgency; a sense that something needs to change now? How are you feeling on the verge of something?

- Keeping in mind that the path to breakthrough is about thriving, not just surviving breakdown, what is the breakthrough you most need in order to fulfill your highest purpose? Think carefully about this but don't overanalyze it.

- As you identify this area of personal breakthrough, write it down, fold up the paper, put it away and don't look at it for a few months. Forget about it. Let it go. Trust that you will manifest the breakthrough you most need, which may or may not be what you wrote on your paper, so instead of getting attached to the outcome you want, simply be in faith that something wonderful is unfolding.

Miracle Experiment: Breaking Through

Relax your body and quiet your thoughts with some deep, slow breaths. Imagine the clear, bright energy of all those others who have ever participated in a miracle experiment, past, present, and future, joining you. We are all vibrating together now in shared consciousness beyond the illusionary limits of space and time, each of us bringing only higher love to the whole. See this joining as beautiful, sacred, awe-inspiring, and filled with the potent energy of love. Open your heart to all of these unseen, unknown friends and shine your love to them.

As a group joined in loving consciousness, we form a powerful network for manifestation and miracles. Recognize how much more powerful we are together. Our joined intentions heighten our magnetism to our highest good. Together, anything is possible. Take a moment to feel the light and energy of our network building.

Now bring to mind your desired breakthrough. Bring it to mind lightly, playfully, knowing that what you envision may or may not be what actually unfolds, because Spirit may have something better in store for you. Just let the imagining be pleasurable. Picture it as having already happened and enjoy walking around in this reality.

Turn this reality over to God in perfect trust that this or something better is now materializing in your life. Let it fly away as easily as a butterfly that lit in your hand, and picture not one but thousands of butterflies taking flight as all the souls in our network, in all places and times, lightly let go with you.

Imagine that out of all the souls in our miracle experiment network, there is one who is particularly ready to break through to a new level of well-being, more so than anyone else. This isn't the person we might agree to be the most broken or needy. This person is ready and able to receive the energy of the whole network and turn it into a life-changing shift, a shift that will not only raise their quality of life but will also powerfully expand this individual's ability to make a positive difference in the world. This is the one best able to spread Unity consciousness through the world. And because we are all connected, this is the person whose transformation will ripple out through time and space as a focused transmission to each one of us, triggering wonderful breakthroughs in the rest of us so that we all rise into our highest good. You don't know who this person is, but you are able to recognize them in your mind's eye by the brightness of their spirit and their receptivity.

As you shine your own love to this soul, you feel it being received by the wave of gratitude and joy that flows back to you. You don't need to believe this is really doing anything, just imagine that you are a miracle-maker, that your love is so powerful it can change someone's life for the better, and that you receive great joy from sharing your gift of miracles.

Imagine this person released from old, limiting patterns that have kept them from fulfilling their purpose in the highest way. Imagine them now living each day in great joy. See them become a beacon to the world around them. See this person actualized in a way that enables them to lead the world toward renewal and harmony. Imagine their breakthrough releasing a seismic vibration throughout the miracle experiment network of souls, becoming a catalyst for new levels of freedom, power and joy for many. Imagine it reaching you, giving you everything you need to achieve your highest good.

Imagine what it might feel like to be this person, whose wake has touched us all. What do you imagine he or she feels flying free from the chains of the past; finding new zest for life; making a positive difference in the world? Imagine it...

Now, imagine that the individual everyone saw as the brightest, the most ready to transform, the one who can take us all the highest... is actually you. You don't need to believe this to be true. Just imagine what it would feel like if you did believe it to be the truth. Would you be pleased? Frightened? Unworthy? Unwilling? Grateful? Just imagine...

Even though no one would ever know, the one to take us all higher could be you. You might not even know for sure yourself, but you just might be that important to all of us. Just imagine...

Exercise for the Day:

As you go about your day, imagine the whole miracle experiment network has recognized in you the readiness to have a breakthrough so significant that your life may never be the same. Feel the faith, love and strength of many with you as you lead us all to where we most need to go.

❖❖❖❖❖❖❖

We're all at a collective crisis point where the work of identifying and transforming all that limits Oneness can't wait. We must undertake it collectively through social activism, and personally through rigorous self-scrutiny and personal growth. This is the only way to catch the wave that's taking humanity higher and avoid being dragged down by all that's falling apart. We've reached a crucial point where, if we are to see humankind move forward into renewal and not extinction, sufficient numbers of us must become activists in the outer world and equally dedicated to our inner lives. We can't create the best possible world without also becoming the best possible human. Waging war against the world's injustices without healing the war within, or retreating from the outer world into a cocoon of self-exploration, are not the options of our new era.

What difference will you choose to make today?

Chapter 18: What's Next: A New Kind of Love

Futurist Jeremy Rifkin traces the historical evolution of humanity's capacity for empathy, correlating it with each significant expansion in communication and transportation and the technology that facilitates these. Beginning with hunter/gatherers whose empathy didn't extend beyond their tribe, to today, he charts a progression of leaps in our ability to bond. He suggests that these leaps have been crucial to our well-being: "The history of the human journey suggests that happiness is not to be found in materialism, but, rather, in empathic engagement."[1] He sees the global network created by the internet ushering in the most profound leap yet in empathic concern: "Empathic sensitivity is expanding laterally as quickly as global networks are connecting everyone together." He goes on, "This transformation is being accompanied by a change in the human psyche—the leap to biosphere consciousness and the Collaborative Age."[2]

In other words, as we evolve our technology, it also evolves us. Through the internet, not only are we starting to act as a global collective, the collective is becoming increasingly personal. For the first time, we are experiencing the interconnectedness of all beings and things, and living life accordingly.

The 1980s saw a proliferation of support and recovery groups that seemed to suggest a "wounded" society. The popularity of such groups may well have been a response to a growing disintegration of community and connection that in another era was taken for granted. Previous generations were less on the move and more likely to live in the same neighborhood, in touch with extended family, knowing and being known over time by a relatively consistent group of people. For better or worse, there was a sense of belonging and identity that came from living in close proximity to our "tribe." But, as society became increasingly mobile and the country more densely populated, by the seventies people could easily live in the same apartment building or on the same street without knowing each other or sharing any sense of connection. It became far easier to live amidst thousands of people and be unknown, unseen, and desperately lonely. The rise of the internet, however, has changed this.

While many argue, with some truth, that the internet has bred a new kind of alienation consisting of relatedness devoid of eye contact, there's no denying that anyone with access to the internet has vast opportunities to connect with other people that were never available before. At the same time that world population is growing, giving us more and more reason to feel invisible and alienated, we now have an extremely personal technology enabling us to reach beyond the chasm of our distance and numbers to touch individuals we'll never meet. Facebook, Twitter, You Tube, and so on are putting a personal face to the vast abstraction of "humanity." Social networks such as Meetup.com and Neighborhood.com are making it easier to meet like-minded others face-to-face and to interact with our neighbors.

Our hearts go out to people in distant corners of the world who we will never meet in person, or to neighbors who we may never encounter walking down the street. On Nextdoor.com, I've experienced much empathy, kindness and helpfulness shared in group discussions among neighbors who I know little about other than they are somewhere nearby. I'm grateful for it.

An interesting example of this new kind of caring occurred around the video "Kony 2012," that quickly went viral in an unprecedented way when it was released in 2012. This thirty-minute long documentary portrayed atrocities being committed by Ugandan war lord Joseph Kony, and received over 100 million views in less than a week—something that had never happened before.

This story drew little attention when it was covered by mainstream media. It took the more personal, one-by-one dissemination of You Tube for people to pay attention in the tens of millions and to experience something heart-felt around these crimes against humanity.

Though the project itself had many flaws and critics, the phenomenon of it illustrates how our technology has primed us for global caring, teaching us how to love in a whole new way, reaching beyond the tribe mentality of local community to break faceless "humanity" down into people, and care deeply—not surprisingly, with millennials leading the way. If you've never heard of "Kony 2012," it may be because you're too old. A Pew Research Center poll suggested that more than half of young adult Americans had heard of it.[3]

In our miracle experiment journey here, we have removed the "training wheels" that the internet has provided for humanity's evolution into One Mindedness and raced at a breakneck pace into kindness, compassion and helpfulness among people who we will never meet face-to-face, using only the communication vehicle of our consciousness and love.

As this book ends, as books must, recognize that our journey together is without end because we have chosen to make this very real connection to untold numbers of hearts and minds. My input has been minimal while yours has created something everlasting in the ever-present NOW. In this last experiment, let us celebrate our creation!

Miracle Experiment: Thank You, Dear Friends

Quiet your mind for a moment and let your attention float free. Take a deep breath or two to help you transition to a soft, open mental state...

Now, imagine yourself on the other side of a life-changing shift. You may not even realize exactly what this shift is. You may not fully believe it. Just imagine that there has been a remarkable change, and you feel great peace around this shift. You may also feel bittersweet in knowing that life as you knew it will never return. You can look back, but you can't turn back. As you reflect on all that's been in your life, give thanks. Know that there have been no mistakes, no failures, because each moment has brought you here, to exactly where you need to be. Take a moment to be alone in this contemplation...

And now let it go, because life is calling you to thrive and you have much to do. You see that you are surrounded by multitudes of other souls who have been with you through this miracle experiment journey, raising you to new levels of opportunity and rooting for your success. Reach out to these souls in joy and love: friends who you will never meet but intimately care about none the less. Know that they will always be with you because of the connection you have made. You will never be alone.

And now you see more souls, stopping to dream at the beginning of their miracle experiment journey. They are stopping to wonder and imagine, just as you once did. You see that some are full of hope and excitement. Others have deep faith and dive into the journey unquestioningly. You see that some are in the midst of pain, confusion, and their own personal dark night of the soul.

Though these souls are new to the journey, your heart recognizes them as old friends. Part of you understands that you have always been together, and you reach out welcoming arms to them.

As they stop to dream with expectant hearts, you wonder if they can feel you cheering them on. You're able to see the most remarkable threshold rising up before them, waiting for them to cross; a threshold that is invisible from their vantage point. You are filled with wonder at the realization that somehow you have already crossed. You may not know exactly how this happened or what this means but you know that it's a glorious thing.

From your heart, now send to these others who are about to join us, the most heartfelt message: Welcome, dear friends! We have been waiting for you. Together, anything is possible! Today we change the world!

Conclusion

I began this book in 2014 with a premise related to the Harmonic Convergence—one that even I thought to be a bit sketchy at the start—pointing to 2016 as being a tipping point in humanity's evolution. For my premise to hold water, I would expect 2016 to be a year full of extremes, having a huge impact on the next twenty-nine years, the next phase of our evolution, and even on our very survival. Over the next couple of years I watched history unfold with my jaw dropped. In spite of my earlier suspicions, I had no idea what was to come.

As I watched the extremes of populist egalitarianism and hierarchical power duke it out in the presidential election in the form of Sanders and Trump, I never expected a Trump presidency. I hoped that the impulse toward Unity would come of age with Bernie Sanders leading us into a new era. That was not to be and, even though I rooted for Hillary and was one of those many in shock on election night to find that she lost, truthfully, the old-school politician with lackluster support who was bound to repeat the obstruction of the Obama administration—in other words, same old, same old—just didn't fit with the pattern of seven-year turning points I saw over the last twenty-nine years: the towers falling on 9/11 of 2001, the Great Recession of 2008, then same old, same old in 2016? Bernie Sanders doing what no one believed he could do might have fit as the end of that story. But so does Trump.

Bernie Sanders and Donald Trump stepped beyond mere politics to portray the paralleling, yin and yang forces of a tipping point era, embodying in very pure and dramatic ways the dueling energies of new and old paradigms. Hillary Clinton, no matter that she won the popular vote and probably would have won the election if not for the many forms of voter suppression in place, for all her experience and competence, simply didn't carry the energy of the times as strongly.

As I complete this writing six months into Trump's presidency, his first 100 days saw failed agendas and growing scandals over Russian connections. In many cases, sheer activism reduced him and his administration to impotence. Now, with formal investigations underway, speculations abound that his term won't last four years.

Was there a reason that we collectively needed to raise Trump to the highest position of leadership in the world and then watch him crash and burn so dramatically? The many ways he has awakened us and brought us together are clear, but what might have become of Trump if he hadn't won the presidency? Would he have quietly gone back to reality TV? Or would he have returned to his new-found comfort zone of rallying adulating crowds of angry, disenchanted white people who loved him during the campaign? Might he have found a solid place as leader of a growing movement of white nationalism that would still be on the rise with the added fury of cheated underdogs, and with ongoing coverage of a media that loves him and the ratings he produces?

Would a Hillary Clinton presidency have enabled the majority of us to go back to sleep, secure in the knowledge that someone competent was at the helm? Would many of us have tuned out, cynical that our vote didn't seem to have any impact on a government stalled in obstruction? And then, instead of a movement reflecting "indivisibility," would the more rapidly growing and impassioned movement be that of white nationalist hate groups? In Europe, nationalism and nationalist candidates gained ground all through Donald Trump's rise in the presidential campaign, but, in the six months following his election, a string of European countries, including Austria, Holland, France and the U.K., all rejected nationalist candidates in their elections, and have growing populist movements. The extremity of our times is causing many to wake up and step up—and for some, this is in service to hate-filled causes, making hate groups more visible than ever. But in spite of this, something has shifted. The sleeping giant of Most of Us has also awakened and become a transformative force of change.

In such unprecedented times, it's hard to speculate on what might have been or what's to come, and even harder to place the last period and end the documenting of these ever-changing times. But perhaps there was an important lesson in the populist Bernie Sanders, and then the competent Hillary Clinton both losing the presidency to a leader of such unprecedented incompetence and unpopularity. Trump's presidency, at least at the time of this writing, seems to be making it dramatically clear that we have no single leader who will save us. And isn't that how it should be in this new era of the collective?

In the midst of all this, is humanity evolving? In my mind, there's not a doubt that we are. Does evolution guarantee, however, that humanity will survive to see another millennium or even another century turn? I would say this is far less certain. Might the wave of so many of us connected and acting together be the force that turns the tide away from the powers of an old age that are fighting so hard against change? Or will a reboot occur as masses of humanity die off from our self-inflicted wounds, leaving a small, wiser group to begin again? Could it be that we, along with much other life on this planet, meet a sudden extinction—the end game of nuclear war or climate shifts?

Even this last catastrophic end may allow a sort of evolution as pure consciousness without physicality. But does this latter path hold some kind of spiritual consequence? In other words, if we use our time here on earth fighting with each other instead of thriving together, and then accidentally destroy ourselves in the process, is there some kind of spiritual make-up work that we will be destined to do?
I'll leave this last question for those wiser than me to speculate on. The other possibilities seem quite real. I don't see any of these outcomes as warranting our fear, yet they do call for our participation. Never has it been so urgent for every individual to actively participate in the well-being of our world.

As you see, my conclusion here is more one of questions than of answers. I even question my own premise: did an evolutionary impulse from outside of us really implant itself in the core of humanity in 1987? Or, perhaps, were the intentions of so many people on that weekend event—an event unprecedented in its magnitude and in its emphasis on community—powerful enough to harness the power of consciousness in an unprecedented way and set in motion a new call to Unity? Was it perhaps the beginning of a global group agreement to evolve? Even with this premise that I've defended throughout these pages, I don't presume to know.

What I do know is that we've never seen times quite like these and, as frightening as some developments appear to be, there are just as many wonderfully hopeful ones. I hope that you, my reader, whether you are reading this in 2018 or decades later, are seeing the fulfillment of seeds planted, not just in 1987 but in the tipping point year of 2016. We are in a new era and, going forward, what happens next is no longer up to "them." It's up to us; to you.

And as never before, the power is in your hands. What will you do with it?

June 19, 2017

Appendix I

1987: Seeds of unity are sown.

- **The first three events to organize world consciousness toward world peace** occurred within months of the Harmonic Convergence:
    o The World Day of Prayer in October of 1986
    o World Peace Day, December 31, 1986
    o The Harmonic Convergence, August 17, 1987

- **The stock market reached a high in August followed by the historic "Black Monday"** crash in October. The crash highlighted the new degree to which financial markets around the world had become connected.

- **In August, Alan Greenspan was appointed Chairman of the Federal Reserve** by Ronald Reagan as Ayn Randian politics of
- selfishness rose in popularity. The effects of this will be felt years later, especially at the 2008 testing point, as Alan Greenspan is considered to have had a significant hand in

engineering the 2008 Great Recession. By 2008, he himself admitted that his financial ideology was flawed.

1987-95 Overview: This first seven-year phase produced the beginnings of a massive, new infrastructure of connection.

This early phase of growth started with a cluster of first ever events to organize world consciousness toward peace. These years were also the incubation phase of internet and cell phone technologies that would soon create a web of connection and communication throughout the world.

A sort of global brain began to form through these new technologies of connection. Simultaneously, the work of a number of scientists began to coalesce into an astonishing new understanding of the Zero Point Field as being the repository of all memory and information rather than the brain. As scientists were beginning to understand how individual minds tap into this universal field of consciousness, individual computers combined with internet technology were evolving into a precise, technological replica of this field. On multiple levels, as a species we were becoming "One-Minded."

1995: This date marks the first testing point as Saturn comes 90 degrees from its position at the Harmonic Convergence.

- **The internet explosion began in 1995.** At this time, the internet was privatized and launched for mass consumption. Netscape and Microsoft introduced the first user-friendly web browsers (the first one going on sale in February, exactly at the precise 90-degree mark), early search engines such as Yahoo! Search were introduced and AOL began signing up private users by the millions. Sprint launched the first text messaging service.

1995-2001 Overview: This second, approximately seven-year phase marks a period of rapid growth before more severe testing occurs.

A short pass of Saturn over the precise 90-degree point in 1995 suggests a quieter phase of development without earth-shattering tests. Yet this period saw a most significant advancement toward unification as the technologies of connection took off. By 2001, the number of adults in the United States using the internet and email crossed the half-way mark. The power and importance of these technologies will become more significant throughout the tests and challenges to come.

2001: Saturn passes over the highly stressful 180-degree mark, bringing a time of severe testing.

- **With the first long pass of Saturn over the crucial degree since 1987, 2001 represents the first great test** of the new age that was birthed at the Harmonic Convergence. On September 11, just days after Saturn makes an exact pass over the precise zodiacal degree, a massive terrorist attack on the United States kills 2,977 people. Planes destroy the Twin Towers in New York City and damage the Pentagon. A third plane is brought down before reaching its target as passengers succeed in overcoming the terrorists aboard.

- **Just a week after the attack, the first of a series of anthrax attacks occurs**, with letters containing anthrax being sent to major media outlets. Twenty-two are exposed and five die, heightening fears of terrorist attacks.

- **On September 20, President George W. Bush declares a "War on Terror."**

- **On October 7, the U.S. invades Afghanistan** with participation from other nations. The Taliban offers to hand over Osama bin Laden to a third country for trial if the U.S. halts the bombing of Afghanistan and provides evidence against him. President Bush rejects the offer, beginning the longest war in U.S. history.

2001-2008 Overview: The third seven-year phase is marked by escalating fear along with the birth of social media as we know it.

This phase began with the world-changing events of 9/11, after which the world gathered in great solidarity and support around the shocked and mourning United States. Vigils were held around the globe and leaders, even of many countries not on friendly terms with the U.S., expressed their sorrow and condemned the act.

This moment of solidarity was short-lived. An era of ever-deepening fear began. People of the United States lost the naïve illusion of invulnerability and our fear of a foreign "Other" sharpened.

A couple of years after 9/11, based on false intelligence, the U.S. and allied nations invaded Iraq, beginning a protracted armed conflict in the region. Destabilizing the already precarious balance of the Middle East led to an increased prevalence of terrorism around the world.

This phase also saw the birth and rise into popularity of social media. The platforms that have most contributed to wide-scale use of social media were launched during these years, including Myspace, Skype, Facebook, You Tube, and Twitter.

2008: Another long pass over the crucial degree at the 270-degree point brings a global financial collapse and the rising stress of opposing forces.

- **In June, Barack Obama becomes the first African American in U.S. history to be nominated** on a major party ticket. He is the first presidential candidate to tap the growing power of social media to organize, inform and fundraise.

- **In September, Lehman Brothers collapses**, starting the serious nose dive of the global economy that becomes known as the Great Recession.

- **Obama wins in November in a landslide victory** with an overwhelming backing of younger voters seeking change from the status quo.

- **Also in the 2008 election, California voters approve a ban on same-sex marriage**—the now-notorious "Prop 8"—taking away marriage rights that had been granted only six months earlier. This reversal of progress mobilizes the gay and gay-allied community in a way that propels nation-wide marriage rights forward far more quickly than anyone expected.

2008-2016 Overview: This last seven-year phase, before Saturn returns to its original position, brings a titanic clash of opposing forces.

Throughout Obama's presidency, Republican lawmakers were unprecedented in their degree of obstructionism. In a secret meeting that took place the day Obama was inaugurated in January 2009, leading Republicans vowed to oppose anything Obama did.[1]

In 2010, two court rulings, including the notorious "Citizens United" Supreme Court ruling, completely rewrote the laws of campaign spending, legalizing unlimited corporate spending on behalf of a candidate. Super PACs came into being and no longer was there any semblance of a level electoral playing field as billions of corporate dollars went toward electing candidates that favored corporate interests.

Much of this new Super PAC money went toward a highly effective Republican strategy to take over government at the local level, which ultimately enabled a web of voter suppression efforts including gerrymandering districts to favor Republicans, imposing restrictive voter I.D. laws, reducing voting stations in heavily Democratic areas, and cross check operations that shaved tens of thousands from voter rolls.

The effects of a depressed economy forced into being innovative forms of collaborative resource sharing, reusing, recycling, and sustainability that began to replace old habits of owning, consuming and disposing.

A millennial generation, the largest generation in Western history and one profoundly shaped both by the internet and the recession, moved from childhood into adulthood, leading trends toward collaboration and connection, primarily through internet platforms. The emergence of a new sharing economy radically changed many industries such as music, publishing, and media as the public increasingly had direct access to a wide range of artists, bloggers and low-cost or free online resources.

A new civil rights movement, in the form of Black Lives Matter, grew up in 2013, following the acquittal of George Zimmerman for the shooting death of African American teen, Trayvon Martin. The movement, protesting systemic racism and brutality by police against African Americans, cast light on an ever-too-frequent occurrence of unwarranted deaths of weaponless and often crimeless African Americans at the hands of police. The new-era prevalence of cell phone videos wrenchingly heightened public awareness of deaths that previously relied only on police officers' recounting of events. Unlike the leader-driven civil rights movement of fifty years earlier, this millennial-heavy movement relies not on charismatic leaders but on grassroots social media.[2]

Internet and cell phone technology, social media, and masses of millennials all come of age at once, providing the necessary ingredients for the "New Operating Model" where individuals are empowered beyond anything we've previously known through small contributions of many into an organizing, internet enabled infrastructure. By 2016, the evolution of this new operating model, along with the countering effect of many threads of established power vying to maintain control, culminate in two unlikely, yet highly popular, presidential candidates: Bernie Sanders and Donald Trump.

2016: Saturn returns to its original position with a long pass over the crucial degree, starting in January and ending around the time of the presidential election, bringing a year of unprecedented extremes.

- **Republican obstructionism takes the unprecedented form** of denying Obama a Supreme Court nominee following the death of Antonin Scalia in early 2016.

- **A volatile stock market begins the year with panic** over the lowest opening since 1897[3], and ends the year at an all-time high. Billionaire Warren Buffet warns of the financial unpredictability of the times.

- **Spurred by the Trump campaign, nationalism is on the rise,** as are white supremacist and hate groups. The Southern Poverty Law Center tracks a marked rise in hate crimes. Nationalism is on the rise throughout Europe as well. Great Britain shocks many with its vote to exit the European Union. This decision is brought into being primarily by older people holding separatist values, the younger generation voting overwhelmingly against it.

- Spurred by, or perhaps simply concurrent with, the Clinton campaign, a spotlight is cast upon women's issues, including sexual assault. High profile offenders are in the news including Bill Cosby, Fox News founder Roger Ailes, and even Donald Trump. Victims who have previously been intimidated into silence are now willing to speak out.

- In October, just one month before the election, the *Access Hollywood* tape of Trump admitting to sexually assaulting women is released. Shortly thereafter, WikiLeaks releases its hacked emails from Hillary Clinton. While it's difficult to say how these releases may have helped either candidate, it's not hard to see how they turned off many voters to both candidates.

- Donald Trump wins the Electoral College. Hillary Clinton wins the popular vote. Trump becomes President Elect.

2017: Past the Tipping Point

As I write this, just half-way through 2017, there are already many signs of an enormous tip toward unification, even as the bad keeps getting worse. Days after Trump took office, the largest and most peaceful worldwide demonstration in history took place: Women's March of January 21, 2017. Masses of people have "awakened" and become politically active, protesting Trump administration policies, inspiring new progressive candidates, and reaching out to marginalized communities. Using the Republican strategy to take over local government, huge numbers of people, many who had never been politically active, began to organize with the help of such movements as "Indivisible" and "Our Revolution." Organized resistance has effectively stopped Republican legislation from passing, including a much-promised overhaul of healthcare

In dramatic contrast to the growth of new, grassroots sharing economies, in 2017, Donald Trump assembled the richest cabinet in American history full of kingpins of mega-industries with flagrant conflicts of interest, promising to further escalate the consequences of unchecked, old-paradigm hierarchical power.

As an unprecedented hurricane season ravaged the southeast and unprecedented firestorms demolished vast areas in the west, Donald Trump's administration rolled back Obama administration environmental protections. Trump withdrew the U.S. from the Paris Agreement on Climate Change Mitigation, making the U.S. the only nonparticipating country in the world.

Trump's poll numbers plummeted giving him the lowest popularity rating of any president in their first year of office.

❖❖❖❖❖❖❖

Here ends my chronicling. The rest of this story is up to you, my friends.

Appendix II

New Leadership Exercise

1. Make time and space to hear your inner guidance. It's been speaking; have you been listening?

2. Break through the resistance of inertia, apathy, ambivalence, avoidance, unconsciousness and fear to do what your heart knows is right.

3. Accept help when it's offered. Reach out for help when it's needed. Recognize that going it alone no longer works.

4. Let others see your vulnerability and imperfections. Let your mask down. Recognize that sometimes it's okay to be "messy."

5. Speak your truth even when doing so is out of your comfort zone. It's time for you to be heard.

6. Find new and more ways to express your creativity. Recognize that your creative imagination is capable of making the world a better place.

7. Let go of your excuses for why you can't, why it's impossible, why it's not your fault or why something else is responsible for your experience. Recognize everything in your world as being a reflection of your own consciousness and therefore within your power to change.

8. Lead by the example of your being rather than by your directions. (Be inspired by who I am rather than by what I tell you to do.)

9. Let go of fear-based control that seeks safety through managing details. Relax, breathe and know that you are safe in the process of life.

10. Make the important decisions that will affect the rest of your life. Let go of procrastination, inertia or choosing by not choosing at all.

11. Be willing to step out into the unknown when inner guidance urges you, even if you can only see the next, immediate step and don't know where the path is taking you.

12. Be willing to let go of certainties, defensiveness, judgments and self-righteousness to allow a bigger picture to emerge—one that recognizes connection rather than differences.

Acknowledgments

Many thanks to my first readers: novelist Billy Parolini, Reverend Deb Teramani, Dr. Sam Bullington and Cherie Anderson. As much as I appreciated their praise, their critical honesty helped immeasurably with the rewriting and polishing that went into this final work.

A big thank you goes to my editor, Alison Williams, who is not only a very capable editor, but is the only person who has ever critiqued my work as a "layperson" not already immersed in my subject matter. It was an invaluable perspective.

I am grateful to Constance Kellough, founder of Namaste Publishing, and publisher of my previous book (*Making Miracles,* also released as *Holding a Butterfly)* for too many things to mention here. Quite simply, she has been a wonderful role model to me.

Thanks to the incredibly talented Alex Baker for help with cover design and so much more. Most of all, my loving gratitude goes to my husband, Bill Baker. His many creative and technical talents, his unconditional support and confidence in me, and his never-flagging love all keep me going in so many ways!

Endnotes

Chapter 2: The Seeds of Change—The Power of Us All Together

1. "About Jose Arguelles/Valum Vaton," *Foundation for the Law of Time,* 2016, http://www.lawoftime.org/infobooth/hc24.html

2. Kimberly Amadeo, "What Is Black Monday? In 1987, 1929, and 2015,*" The Balance*, Updated October 14, 2016, https://www.thebalance.com/what-is-black-monday-in-1987-1929-and-2015-3305818

3. Donald Bernhardt and Marshall Eckblad, "Black Monday: The Stock Market Crash of 1987," *The Federal Reserve History*, November 22, 2013, http://www.federalreservehistory.org/Events/DetailView/48

4. Maureen Dowd, "'Where Atlas Shrugged' is still read—Forthrightly," *New York Times*, September 13, 1987, http://www.nytimes.com/1987/09/13/weekinreview/where-atlas-shrugged-is-still-read-forthrightly.html

5. Clifford Stoll, "Why the Web Won't Be Nirvana," *Newsweek*, February 26, 1995, http://www.newsweek.com/clifford-stoll-why-web-wont-be-nirvana-185306

6. Yue Wang, "More People Have Cell Phones than Toilets, U.N. Study Shows," *Time*, March 25, 2013, http://newsfeed.time.com/2013/03/25/more-people-have-cell-phones-than-toilets-u-n-study-shows/

7. Pierre Teilhard de Chardin, *The Phenomenon of Man* (New York: Harper Colophon, 1975), 244.

8. Ralph Abraham, *"The Mycelial Mat and the World Wide Web,"* Lecture, Telluride Mushroom Festival and Conference, Telluride, CO, August 1995.http://www.ralph-abraham.org/talks/transcripts/mycelial.txt

9. Lisa Gansky, *The Mesh* (London: Penguin Books Ltd, 2010).

10. Kurt Andersen, "The Protester," *Time,* December 14, 2011, http://content.time.com/time/specials/packages/article/0,28804,2101745_2102132,00.html

11. Frank Richaug, "The Billionaires Bankrolling the Tea Party," *New York Times*, August 28, 2010, http://www.nytimes.com/2010/08/29/opinion/29rich.html

12. Bruce Lipton, *Spontaneous Evolution* (Carlsbad: Hay House, 2009), xxii.

Chapter 3: The Point of Breakdown or Breakthrough

1. Nicholas St. Fleur, "Where in the World Is Climate Change Denial Most Prevalent?" *New York Times*, December 11, 2015, https://www.nytimes.com/interactive/projects/cp/climate/2015-paris-climate-talks/where-in-the-world-is-climate-denial-most-prevalent

2. Chris Mooney, "The Strange Relationship between Global Warming and... Speaking English," *The Guardian*, July 23, 2014, https://www.theguardian.com/environment/2014/jul/23/the-strange-relationship-between-global-warming-denial-and-speaking-english

3. Bruce Schneier, "Beyond Security Theater," *New Internationalist*, November 2009, https://www.schneier.com/essays/archives/2009/11/beyond_security_thea.html

4. Sarah Lazare, "Body Count Report Reveals At Least 1.3 Million Lives Lost to US-Led War on Terror," *Global Research*, March 31, 2015, https://www.globalresearch.ca/body-count-report-reveals-at-least-1-3-million-lives-lost-to-us-led-war-on-terror/5439827

5. The Editorial Board, "The Most Extreme Republican Platform in Memory," *New York Times*, July 18, 2016, https://www.nytimes.com/2016/07/19/opinion/the-most-extreme-republican-platform-in-memory.html?_r=0

6. Katrina vanden Heuval, "The most progressive Democratic platform ever," *Washington Post*, July 12, 2016, https://www.washingtonpost.com/opinions/the-most-progressive-democratic-platform-ever/2016/07/12/82525ab0-479b-11e6-bdb9-701687974517_story.html?utm_term=.d3235d963cc9

7. Jenna Johnson, "Donald Trump: They say I could 'shoot somebody' and still have support," *Washington Post*, January 23, 2016,

https://www.washingtonpost.com/news/post-politics/wp/2016/01/23/donald-trump-i-could-shoot-somebody-and-still-have-support/?utm_term=.b921dddc8880

8. Ian Samples, "Rising deaths among white middle-aged Americans could exceed Aids toll in US," *The Guardian*, November 2, 2015, https://www.theguardian.com/science/2015/nov/02/death-rate-middle-aged-white-americans-aids

9. Chris McGreal, "Financial Despair, Addiction and the Rise of Suicide in White America," *The Guardian*, February 7, 2016, https://www.theguardian.com/us-news/2016/feb/07/suicide-rates-rise-butte-montana-princeton-study

10. Mark Potok, "The Year in Hate and Extremism," *Southern Poverty Law Center*, February 17, 2016, https://www.splcenter.org/fighting-hate/intelligence-report/2016/year-hate-and-extremism

11. Maureen B. Costello, Richard Cohen, ed. "The Trump Effect: The Impact of the Presidential Election on our Nation's Schools," *Southern Poverty Law Center,* November 28, 2016, https://www.splcenter.org/20161128/trump-effect-impact-2016-presidential-election-our-nations-schools

12. Greg Palast, "The GOP's Stealth War Against Voters," *Rolling Stone*, August 24, 2016, http://www.rollingstone.com/politics/features/the-gops-stealth-war-against-voters-w435890

13. Paul Bond, "Leslie Moonves on Donald Trump: 'It May Not Be Good for America, but It's Damn Good for CBS,'" *The Hollywood Reporter*, February 29, 2016, http://www.hollywoodreporter.com/news/leslie-moonves-donald-trump-may-871464

14. Barbara Kollmeyer, "'Rich Dad' author says the 2016 market collapse he foresaw in 2002 is coming," *Market Watch*, March 28, 2016, http://www.marketwatch.com/story/rich-dad-author-says-the-market-collapse-he-foresaw-in-2002-is-coming-2016-03-23

15. John Minnich, "China's economic problems will come to a head in 2017," *Market Watch*, November 23, 2016, http://www.marketwatch.com/story/chinas-economic-problems-will-come-to-a-head-in-2017-2016-11-23

16. Warren Buffet, Berkshire Hathaway letter to shareholders, February 27, 2016, http://www.berkshirehathaway.com/letters/2015ltr.pdf,

Chapter 6: "Thrival" as the Path to Survival

1. Bruce Lipton, *Spontaneous Evolution* (Carlsbad: Hay House, 2009),122-126.

2. Jonas Ellison, "Don't Compete—Create," *Huffington Post*, Nov 15, 2016, http://www.huffingtonpost.com/jonas-ellison/dont-compete-create_b_8572296.html

Chapter 7: What did we just do? The Elements of a New Spiritual Practice

1. Rupert Sheldrake, "Morphic Resonance and Morphic Fields - an Introduction," *Sheldrake.org, 2016,*

https://sheldrake.org/research/morphic-
resonance/introduction?highlight=WyJyZXNvbmFuY2UiLCJtb3JwaGljIi
wibW9ycGhpYyIsImZpZWxkcyIsImFuIiwiaW50cm9kdWN0aW9uIiwib
W9ycGhpYyBmaWVsZHMiLCJtb3JwaGljIGZpZWxkcyBhbiIsImZpZWx
kcyBhbiIsImZpZWxkcyBhbiBpbnRyb2R1Y3Rpb24iLCJhbiBpbnRyb2R1
Y3Rpb24iXQ==

2. Lynne McTaggart, *The Bond* (New York: Simon & Schuster, 2011),
178.

3. Lynne McTaggart, *The Intention Experiment* (New York: Simon &
Schuster, 2007), 195.

4. Lynn Woodland, Making *Miracles* (Vancourver, B.C.: Namaste
Publishing, 2011), 8.

5. Larry Dossey, *Be Careful What You Pray For... You Just Might Get It*
(New York: HarperCollins, 1998), 214.

Chapter 8 Compassionate Empathy

1. Lynne McTaggart, *The Field* (New York: HarperCollins, 2002), 185.

2. Lawrence LeShan, *The Medium, the Mystic, and the Physicist* (New
York: Ballantine Books, 1975), 107.

3. LeShan, *The Medium, the Mystic, and the Physicist,* 107.

4. C. D. Bateson et al., "Perspective Taking: Imagining How Another
Feels versus Imagining How You Would Feel," *Personality and Social
Personality Bulletin* 23 (1997): 751-58

5. A. Lutz, et al., "Long-term meditators self-induce high-amplitude gamma synchrony during mental practice," Proceedings of the National Academy of Science, 2004; 101 (46): 16369-73

Chapter Nine: Healing the Duality of Giving and Receiving

1. McTaggart, *The Bond,* 105.

2. Dossey, Larry, *One Mind*, (USA: Hay House, 2013),7.

Chapter Eleven: Collective Intelligence

1. MIT Center for Collective Intelligence, Home Page, 2016, *http://cci.mit.edu/*

2. "A Conversation with Thomas W. Malone," *Edge.org*, Nov. 21, 2012, https://www.edge.org/conversation/thomas_w__malone-collective-intelligence

3. McTaggart, *The Field,* 95.

4. Dossey, *One Mind*, xxiv.

5. Dossey, *One Mind*, xxii.

6. Dossey, *One Mind*, xxx.

7. Quinn Norton, "How Anonymous Picks Targets, Launches Attacks, and Takes Powerful Organizations Down," *Wired,* July 3, 2012, https://www.wired.com/2012/07/ff_anonymous/

Chapter Twelve: Beyond Time and Space

1. McTaggart, *The Intention Experiment*, 170.

2. McTaggart, *The Intention Experiment*, 164.

3. William Braud, PhD, "Wellness Implications of Retroactive Influence: Exploring an Outrageous Hypothesis," *Alternative Therapies in Health and Medicine,* 2000; 6(1): 37-48

4. Woodland, *Making Miracles*, 154.

Chapter Thirteen: New Prosperity

1. Rifkin, Jeremy, *Zero Marginal Cost Society* (New York: Palgrave Macmillan Trade, 2015), 23-24

2. Lewis Mehl-Madrona, M.D., "How to Deal with Depression in the Face of the Holiday Season, and How to Heal." Interviewed by Thom Hartmann, Thom Hartmann Program, Air America Media, December 18, 2008, Transcribed by Caleb Burns, https://www.thomhartmann.com/solr/How%20to%20Deal%20with%20De pression%20in%20the%20Face%20of%20the%20Holiday%20Season%2C %20and%20How%20to%20Heal

Chapter Fourteen: Bringing the Towers Down

1. Scott Heiferman, "9/11 & Us," *The Meetup Blog*, September 10, 2011, http://blog.meetup.com/911-us/

Chapter Fifteen: Healing the Collective Shadow of our Times

1. Cassie Miller, Alexandra Werner-Winslow, "Ten Days After: Harassment and Intimidation in the Aftermath of an Election," *Southern Poverty Law Center, cplcenter.org,* November 29, 2016, https://www.splcenter.org/20161129/ten-days-after-harassment-and-intimidation-aftermath-election

2. Farhad Manjoo, "I Ignored Trump News for a Week. Here's What I Learned," *New York Times,* February 22, 2017, https://www.nytimes.com/2017/02/22/technology/trump-news-media-ignore.html

3. Carl G. Jung, ed. *Man and His Symbols,* (U.S.A.: Dell Publishing, 1968), 181-182.

4. Headlines, "Hundreds of Reports of Racist Attacks in Wake of Trump Victory," *Democracy Now!,* November 11, 2016, https://www.democracynow.org/2016/11/11/headlines/hundreds_of_reports_of_racist_attacks_in_wake_of_trump_victory

Chapter Sixteen: Rising Above Fear

1. Carolyn Miller, *Creating Miracles,* (Tiburon: H. J. Kramer, 1995).

2. American Psychological Association (2017), "Stress in America: Coping with Change," Stress in America™ Survey, February 15, 2017, *apa.org,* http://www.apa.org/news/press/releases/stress/2016/coping-with-change.pdf

3. Linda Dillon, "The Mother's Tsunami of One—Maree & Anastasia," *Counciloflove.com,* June 24, 2016, http://counciloflove.com/2016/06/the-mothers-tsunami-of-one-maree-anastasia/

Chapter Seventeen: All Together Now—Breaking Through

1. Alexa Ura and Alex Samuels, "At Texas Muslim Capitol Day, supporters form human shield around demonstrators," *The Texas Tribune*, January 31, 2017, https://www.texastribune.org/2017/01/31/texas-capitol-rally-muslim-advocacy-day-draws-1000/

Chapter Eighteen: What's Next: A New Kind of Love

1. Rifkin, *Zero Marginal Cost Society*, 368.

2. Rifkin, *Zero Marginal Cost Society*, 370.

3. Rainie, Lee, Hitlin, Paul, Jurkowitz, Mark, Dimock, Michael, Neidorf, Shawn, "The Viral Kony 2012 Video," Washington, D.C.: Pew Research Center, Pewinternet.org, March 15, 2012, http://www.pewinternet.org/2012/03/15/the-viral-kony-2012-video/

Appendix I

1. Ewin MacAskill, "Democrats condemn GOP's plot to obstruct Obama as 'appalling and sad,'" *The Guardian*, April 26, 2012, https://www.theguardian.com/world/2012/apr/26/democrats-gop-plot-obstruct-obama

2. Gene Demby, "The Birth of a New Civil Rights Movement," *Politico Magazine*, December 31, 2014, https://www.politico.com/magazine/story/2014/12/ferguson-new-civil-rights-movement-113906

3. Matt Egan, "Wild January Stock Market Ends on a High Note," *CNN Money*, January 31, 2016, http://money.cnn.com/2016/01/29/investing/dow-january-2016-worst-month/index.html

To You, the Reader:

The Breakthrough Point invites you to reach out in loving consciousness to every other person reading this book as a means of creating new realities for our lives and our world. The book is merely an infrastructure for bringing us all together and, just as Wikipedia would be nothing without its many contributors, so this book is really all about you.

The exercises in *The Breakthrough Point* grow in strength as more of us participate, so if you have felt touched by what you've experienced here, please consider leaving a review on Amazon and sharing this book with your friends and on social media. Together, we can create a new world!

To access recordings of the meditations in this book or to participate in online events with Lynn Woodland, see www.lynnwoodland.com.

Send your comments or subscribe to Lynn Woodland's email bulletins by writing to lynn@lynnwoodland.com.

About *Holding a Butterfly—An Experiment in Miracle-Making*

By Lynn Woodland

(Previously released as *Making Miracles*)

Holding a Butterfly is about consciousness, time, quantum science, and God all woven into a series of practical, personal exercises in miracle-making. It will sweep you up in a collaborative experiment in consciousness that is sure to bend your mind, touch your heart, and forever change reality as you've known it. What can you personally expect from *Holding a Butterfly*? Be open to no less than the fulfillment of your dreams—just don't expect the expected! Miracles awaken us to dreams we never thought to dream before, things our heart has always longed for but our mind has never known how to name, and these may compel us to leave predictability behind. Curious? Come join the experiment—it may just change your life!

What readers say about *Holding a Butterfly*

Just when you think you know a lot about the law of attraction and quantum physics, you read a book like Holding a Butterfly that really pushes your reality and current belief systems to new frontiers.

—Annette Epifano, *New Connexion Journal for Conscious Living*

This may well be the 21st century edition of A Course in Miracles.

—Jim Jensen, author of *Beyond the Power of Your Subconscious Mind*

In considering the depth of some of her exercises, Woodland's genius shines in both their originality and the sense of comfort and possibility they impart, as well as the broad-minded, dumbfoundingly comprehensive approach to putting all this material together and making it fit.

—*Creations Magazine*

[Holding A Butterfly] has very important information to share. (Thanks for writing it...) I read a chapter a night before going to sleep and now will reread it again (which is a very, very rare occurrence for me). I found it very empowering (and I've read a lot of "personal growth" and metaphysical books in the past 25 years). Yours stands out from the pack.

—Marie T. Russell, Editor/Publisher, *Innerself.com*

I have read this book over and over. Because every time I read it miracles continually happen. Over the past 20 years I must have read hundreds of new age books. Forget them all. This is an easy read and the best. H.

If you are willing to participate fully, this book will change you. Highly recommended. K.D.S.

...one of the most important reading[s] of the new era. IT WORKS! Miracles are natural. G.A.

I feel this is one of the best books ever written on miracle-making, manifesting, and connecting with the divine. Truly ground-breaking work, and recommend it to all!! M.K.

I was a bit skeptical about the magnitude of miracles possible. Before I even finished reading the whole book I experienced unimaginable results. W.H.

It is very readable, probably some of the best writing in this genre I have ever experienced. C.S.

Elegantly simple. D.

www.ingramcontent.com/pod-product-compliance
Lightning Source LLC
Chambersburg PA
CBHW031831090426
42741CB00005B/204